A Concise History of the US Airborne

Army, Corps, Divisions and Brigades

with

Lineage and Insignia

by Geoffrey T. Barker

With an Introduction by
Lieutenant General Carl W. Stiner, USA,
Commanding General, XVIII Airborne Corps

ACKNOWLEDGEMENTS

I wish to acknowledge the encouragement, support and assistance, freely provided by the following personnel in their specific areas of expertise:

SFC Frank Eglivitch; LTC Darrell G. Elmore; CW2 Steve Manhart; CW3 Peter McDermott; SFC Gordon L. Rottman; Col Donald J. Soland; LTC (Ret) Jay Massaro (American Society of Military Insignia Collectors); Mr Tim Moriarty, Mr Hubert Snyder (Snyder Enterprises); Mr Romano Danysh and Mr John B. Wilson (US Center of Military History); Mr Ron Woolsey; and the Public Affairs Office, XVIII Airborne Corps. I am especially grateful to my wife Judy - my personal Chief of Staff, whose tremendous enthusiasm and support has been magnificent.

The author welcomes comments or recommendations for changes, additions, or deletions to be included in future editions of this publication. Correspondence may be forwarded through the Anglo-American Publishing Company.

GTB

DEDICATION

The true Airborne Trooper knows exactly how 1,000 'Attaboys' can be quickly counteracted; how major commands can logically prove that 'garbage' flows <u>uphill</u>; and regardless of countless assurances by higher headquarters - there will be no trucks waiting on the Drop Zone.... This volume is dedicated to all "staff pukes" at brigade and higher, who have survived despite often unwarranted criticism, and whose proven support and outstanding dedication has enhanced the entire airborne community.

CONTENTS

INTRODUCTION

Last year, prior to relinquishing command of the 82d Airborne Division to assum
command of the XVIII Airborne Corps, I was talking to Geoff Barker at a function of the Militar
Affairs Commitee of the Fayetteville, North Carolina, Chamber of Commerce. As we discussed hi
book, A Concise History of US Army Special Operations Forces, I asked Geoff if he had considere
compiling a similar concise history of the 82d Airborne Division. He quickly explained th
complexity of such a task, based upon a half century of reorganizations, reassignments an
realignments of the subordinate elements of the Division. Prior to the reorganization of the US Arm
Regimental System, battalions within the same regiment were habitually reassigned between differ
ent divisions, causing a loss of regimental integrity. This convolution could confuse even the mos
hardened military historian, when examining the organization of a single division. The propose
outline of the Concise History Series of US Army airborne forces provides a logical progression fo
the enormous undertaking to document the finest fighting forces of the US Army.

The XVIII Airborne Corps is a strategic force, and is the contingency corps of today
army. The rapid striking abilities of corps assets were demonstrated during the Dominican Republi
crisis in 1965, during Operation URGENT FURY in Grenada in 1983, and again during Operatio
GOLDEN PHEASANT in Honduras in 1988. The capabilities of the XVIII Airborne Corps ar
continually being refined during ongoing exercises in Europe, South West Asia, the Middle Eas
Central America and within the United States. I am proudly confidant in the dedication, th
professional competetance, and the combat readiness of the soldiers assigned to every unit withi
this command.

I look forward to the continuing saga of the American airborne soldiers in the Concise Histor
Series. I am especially pleased to note that unit honors and accomplishments have been included i
the lineage portions of each organization. As we continue to progress forward, we must alway
remember the accomplishments of our predecessors who led the way, and upon whose accomplish
ments our magnificent airborne heritage was built. It is appropriate that our heritage be recorded i
this Concise History series as we celebrate our fiftieth anniversary of the US Army Airborne force:

Carl W. Stiner
Lieutenant General, USA
Fort Bragg, North Carolina

April 1989

Lieutenant General Stiner was born in La Follette, Tennessee, graduating from the Tennesse
Polytechnical Institute with a Bachelor of Science Degree in Agriculture. He earned his Masters Degre
in Public Administration from Shippensburg State College, Pennsylvania. His military educatio
includes the Infantry Basic and Advanced Courses, the Command and General Staff College, and th
US Army War College. Prior to commanding the XVIII Airborne Corps, LTG Stiner commanded th
82d Airborne Division; the Joint Special Operations Command; and served as the Chief of Staff of th
Joint Rapid Deployment Task Force. His many awards and decorations include the Defense Distir
guished Service Medal (with OLC); the Disdtinguished Service Medal; Defense Superior Servic
Medal; Legion of Merit (with OLC); Purple Heart (with OLC); Combat Infantryman's Badge; Maste
Parachutist Badge; Ranger Tab; Army General Staff Identification Badge; and the Joint Chiefs o
Staff Service Badge. LTG Stiner is married to the former Sue Reeves, they have two children, Carl
and Laurie..

Chapter One

The Birth of US Army Airborne Forces

The visionary ideologies of **Brigadier General Billy Mitchell** were not too advanced for the US Army during the 1918 era of World War I. He envisioned a terminal offensive for the war, culminating in a parachute assault by the US **1st Infantry Division** into the German city of Mentz. **Major Lewis H. Brereton** was assigned by **General Jack Pershing** to perform the initial feasibility studies on the use and practicality of airborne forces. The preliminary training and logistical procurement was well underway when the War-to-End-all-Wars finished.

Following WW I, **BG Mitchell** continued to pursue his efforts to introduce parachute troops into the US Army inventory. His untiring efforts influenced the War Department to recommend to **General Lynch**, Chief of Infantry, to formulate the establishment of the **Air Infantry**. The Irvin Company, (who later supplied the British Airborne Forces), filled the initial requisition for parachutes for the US Army parachute troops. A field test site was activated at **McCook Field, Ohio**. Despite feverish advancements by other armed forces throughout the world, the move towards adoption of airborne forces in the US Army was pitifully slow until 1940. It was then that US Army Chief of Staff, **General George C. Marshall**, directed that studies for airborne forces be reconsidered. Needless to say, US involvement in WW II was looming on the immediate military horizon.

Major William C. Lee was assigned the project to implement the results of the voluminous parachute feasibility studies. It was through the steadfast determination and ingenuity of **Major Lee** that aircraft were acquired, parachutes were tested and techniques developed, and that eventually gliders were introduced into the airborne inventory. It was inevitable that **Major Lee** would later receive the enviable title of **Father of the US Airborne.** He progressed further than he ever anticipated, to later command the US **101st Airborne Division.**

The **Parachute Test Platoon** was activated in 1940 at Fort Benning, Georgia from 48 selectees of the more than 200 volunteers from the **29th Infantry Regiment** - supporting the Infantry Board. The **Parachute Test Platoon**, commanded by **Lieutenant William T. Ryder**, was assigned to the Infantry Board. **Lt Ryder** assumed the responsibilities for the basic research, development and testing of parachute equipment, techniques and doctrine. He is credited with designing the circular cloth parachute insignia worn by early parachute troops on the overseas cap. This insignia was the fore-runner of the traditional 'glider patch' worn by personnel on jump-status prior to the adoption of the now familiar airborne maroon beret.

The British airborne school, the **Central Landing School,** was established at Ringway Airport, Manchester. The methods employed to exit the six Whitley aircraft (begrudgingly provided by the Royal Air Force), consisted of either the aperture, (jumping through the hole), or the 'pull-off' method from the tail gunner's position. The first official descent, using the 'pull-off' method was made on 13 July 1940.

History was made on 14 August 1940, when the **Test Platoon** became the first US Army unit to conduct an airborne test exercise, from a Douglas B-18 Aircraft at 1,500 feet. The Commander, **Lt Ryder**, led the way. The enlisted man scheduled to be the first jumper, froze in the door, making way for the number two man - **Private William N. (Red) King**, to become the first enlisted parachutist in the United States Army. Regretfully, **Red King** passed away in September 1988, missing the 50th Anniversay celebrations, scheduled for July 1990 in Washington, DC.

The month following their epic qualifying jump, the **Parachute Test Platoon** became the embryo of the **1st Parachute Battalion.** Later that same month (September 1940), the **1st Parachute Battalion** was redesignated from it's logical nomenclature, to become the **501st Parachute Battalion.** The US Army already enjoyed a notoriety for reorganizing, redesignating and changing the component status of units. This became the precedent for creating the turmoil with the heritage and lineages of airborne and elite units for the next half century. **Major William M. Miley,** the first commander of the **501st Parachute Battalion**, was assigned in November 1940.

The traditional US paratrooper exit cry of **Geronimo**, is attributed to **Private Aubrey Eberhardt**, following the viewing of a western movie the previous evening.

These were dynamic times. The erecting of the landmark 250-foot jump towers commenced at Fort Benning, Georgia in late 1940, as parachute training became an accepted reality within the US Army. The 250-foot towers, designed by the **Safe Parachute Company**, had been a highlight of the 1939 World's Fair held in New York. **Lt Ryder** was promoted to Captain as he continued to refine his earlier parachute training standards and operating procedures. Another stalwart forefather of the US Army airborne community, (later to command the **US Army Special Warfare School** at Fort Bragg, and eventually retire as a Lieutenant General), was **Captain William P. Yarborough**. It was **Captain Yarborough** who designed the Model 1941 US Paratrooper jump suit, the hightopped paratrooper boots, and the distinctive unit insignia (DUI) of the **501st Parachute Battalion**.

In March 1941, the first unit award of the US Army Parachute Badge was made by (then) **Brigadier General Omar N. Bradley**, (later to become General of the Army), Commanding the **US Army Infantry School** at Fort Benning, Georgia. The US Army parachute badge, as still worn today, was designed by none other than that veteran airborne magician - **Captain Bill Yarborough**, who continually made many valuable and innovative contributions on behalf of the airbone community over the years to come. A limiting restriction imposed on **Captain Yarborough** during his design of the parachute badge, was an overall width to be no more than two inches, (to ensure no confusion existed between the wings of a mere parachutist and the revered wings of an aviator). Even these restrictions did not compare with those imposed upon their British airborne counterparts. In order to alleviate any confusion with the wings of the **Royal Air Force**, parachutists wings were (and still continue), to be worn sewn on the upper right uniform sleeve.

Undaunted, **Captain Yarborough** personally hand carried the approved design to a jewelry manufacturer in Philadelphia. He literally camped on the doorstep of **Bailey, Banks and Biddle**, until the initial order of 350 wings were ready for delivery back to Fort Benning. Careful insignia collectors will note the *Triple-B* trademark of Bailey, Banks and Biddle on the back of those newly manufactured items.

Later in 1941, the **Provisional Parachute Group** was activated under (then) **Lieutenant Colonel Bill Lee**, to function as the overall command for the parachute battalion(s) and the parachute school. The **Provisional Parachute Group** was redesignated as the **Airborne Command** in 1941, assuming the proponencies started by the original **Parachute Test Platoon** - developing equipment, doctrine, procedures, training and organizational Tables of Distribution and Allowances (TDA). The nomenclature **Airborne Command**, was adopted over **Parachute Command**, as the command would include glider and artillery units in additional to the traditional parachute infantry organizations.

Within six months, the **502d, 503d** and **504th Parachute Infantry Battalions** had joined the 501st **Parachute Infantry Battalion** under the **Airborne Command**, all stemming from the cadre of the original 1st **Parachute Battalion**. Quickly following, came another breed of airborne soldiers - the **88th and 550th Glider Infantry Battalions** breaking ground for the intrepid glider-borne troops. It should be noted, that whereas parachutists were required to volunteer, the glider soldier was assigned to the duty (either voluntarily or involuntarily).

As the United States drew closer to involvement in World War II, the **501st, 502d** and **503d Parachute Infantry Battalions** were respectively redesignated as the **1st Battalions, 501st, 502d** and **503d Parachute Infantry Regiments**. The **504th Parachute Infantry Battalion** was redesignated as the **2d Battalion, 503d Parachute Infantry Regiment** - and so the confusion began ! The official lineage of the **504th Parachute Infantry Regiment** did not commence (as logic would suppose), with the **504th Parachute Infantry Battalion**, but is not recorded as commencing until the following year in 1942. During that period, the Tables of Organization and Equipment (TO&E), authorized three battalions per parachute infantry regiment, and two battalions for each glider infantry regiment.

Lieutenant General (Ret) William P. Yarborough clarified that the original intent of the wing background worn behind the US Army parachute wings, was an answer to enlarge the appearance of the wings.

Oval backgrounds were not worn behind glider badges. In later years, the wing background oval signified that the wearer of the parachute badge, in addition to being airborne qualified, was currently assigned to a duty parachute position. Prior to the adoption of the airborne maroon beret by the US Army for wear by airborne units, the designs of the ovals indicated to which airborne organization the soldier was assigned, when worn behind the wings on the field cap. The unit is now also identified by the design of the beret flash.

Another innovative tradition started by (then) **Brigadier General Yarborough**, as Commander of **Special Forces** at Fort Bragg, was for each **Special Forces Group** to wear a different 'flash' on the green beret to provide esprit de corps through the visual identification of each Group through the different designs of the flashes. (All **Special Forces Groups** wear the distinctive unit insignia (DUI) of the **1st Special Forces Regiment**). **Brigadier General Yarborough** led his **Special Forces** soldiers past **President John F. Kennedy** at Fort Bragg in 1961 wearing their berets. This was the final turning point for the official adoption of the green beret for US Army **Special Forces.**

During the first half century since the innovation of parachute troops, the US Airborne Forces have increased and declined following World War II. The following chapters reflect some of those changes down to the Brigade level. US Army Special Operations Forces (SOF), are included in Volume 1 of the Concise History Series - **A Concise History of US Army Special Operations Forces.** US Army SOF include **Special Forces, Rangers, Civil Affairs, Psychological Operations** and **Special Operations Aviation, Chemical, Intelligence, Medical, Training** and **Support units.**

US Army Master Parachutist Badge
(with two stars signifying two combat parachute assaults)

Senior Parachutist Badge

Novice Parachutist Badge

Chapter Two

Overview of US Army Airborne Forces

The training of US Army Paratroopers commenced as a confirmed reality in 1940. The **Parachute Test Platoon** was activated and redesignated consecutively as the **1st Parachute Battalion**, then as the **501st Parachute Battalion**. The **501st Parachute Battalion** became the nucleus for the **501st, 502d, 503d and 504th Parachute Infantry Battalions,** which in turn were reorganized and redesignated as the **501st through 504th Parachute Infantry Regiments.** The **501st Parachute Battalion** also provided cadre for the **Provisional Parachute Group,** which was later redesignated as the **Airborne Command.** The history, lineage and insignia of the Parachute, Glider and Airborne Infantry Regiments are contained in Volume 3 of the Concise History Series - <u>A Concise History of US Army Airborne Infantry.</u>

In March 1942, the **82d Division** of the US Army Organized Reserves, was ordered into Active Military Service, to be reorganized and redesignated that following August as the **82d Airborne Division.** Also in August, the **101st Division** was disbanded in the Organized Reserves, and reconstituted in the Army of the United States (AUS), as the **101st Airborne Division.** The **11th, 13th and 17th Airborne Divisions,** also constituted in 1942, were not activated until 1943. The **15th Airborne Division** was constituted in 1944, but not activated.

The United States entered World War II in 1943, with the **82d Airborne Division** deploying in April to the European Theater of Operations (ETO). The **101st Airborne Division** followed in September. Twelve months later, in April 1944, the **11th Airborne Division** embarked to the Pacific Theater. The **17th Airborne Division** deployed to the ETO later in 1944. In January 1945, the **13th Airborne Division** was reassigned from the **Airborne Command** at Camp MacCall, North Carolina, joining the three Airborne Divisions already assigned to the ETO.

The **1st Troop Carrier Command** was organized in 1942 at Stout Field, Indiana, from carrier units of the **Air Transport Command.** The primary functions of the **Troop Carrier Command** included the organizing and training of glider, medical evacuation and troop carrier crews, preparatory to those units being further reassigned to combat commands. Two variations of shoulder sleeve insignia are illustrated for the **1st Troop Carrier Command** The official SSI included the arc with **'I Troop Carrier Command'** above the standard **Army Air Corps** circular insignia. The arc was approved in 1945. Prior to approval of the arc, a popular SSI was locally manufactured depicting a paratrooper being carried by an eagle, with the motto **'Vincit Qui Primum Gerit'** (He Conquors Who Gets There First). This latter unofficial SSI was adapted from the fuselage markings of their aircraft. **The Airborne Troop Carrier** SSI, was similarly not War Department approved, but were worn by the **Airborne Troop Carrier** crews under local authorization. The **317th** and **440th Troop Carrier Groups** of the **Airborne Troop Carrier Command,** participated in every major airborne operation involving US airborne forces, and was involved in many infiltration flights of **Office of Strategic Services** (OSS) personnel.

Prior to the Normandy Landings, the largest deception plan ever attempted, was successfully executed by the Allied forces. Misinformation concerning the 'activation' of fifty non-existent Divisions, was carefully leaked to the Axis Forces as part of Operation **QUICKSILVER.** Included in this 'paper' army were five US Airborne Divisions - the **6th, 9th, 18th, 21st and 135th Airborne Divisions.** These units were part of the ficticious assault into the Pas de Calais coastal region of France, which successfully diverted German forces from Normandy. Shoulder sleeve insignia was actually approved and manufactured as part of this classic deception plan. It should be noted that the **108th Infantry Division,** initially a ficticious unit under Operation **QUICKSILVER,** was actually activated in 1946 as the **108th Airborne Division** in the Organized Reserves.

A little discussed, but extremely highly efficient organization, was the **IX Engineer Command HQ**, organized in the UnIted Kingdom in 1944 as a component of the **9th Air Force.** In addition to commanding four aviation regiments, this headquarters also commanded three airborne and one camouflage aviation engineer battalion. The three airborne battalions were the **876th, 877th** and **878th Aviation Engineer Battalions,** whose mission was to rapidly assault, capture and repair essential airfield facilities within supporting distance of the forward lines. The **IX Engineer Command** SSI was approved for local wear in 1945. Personnel assigned to the airborne aviation engineer battalions were authorized to locally wear the red and white, (Engineer colors), airborne tab.

The airborne soldier made a lasting, indelible mark, in the annals of warfare concepts during the second world war; to be perpetuated in all ensuing battles and conflicts around the globe. He became the most respected and highly feared individual adversary in the field of battle. For fifty years the airborne legacy has been retained, upheld and cherished. Although gliderborne troops have been long discontinued , their contributions were legion. Todays paratrooper deservedly stands tall in the forefront, with other elite forces, ably representing his entire airborne heritage.

Estimations of enemy losses dyring World War II, made it inevitable that, as post-war planning and training commenced, the War Department retain it's airborne capabilities within the US Army. With no regard forf the logic for retention, the **Airborne Command** and the **13th** , **17th** and **101st Airborne Divisions** were inactivated during 1945-1946. The **XVIII Corps (Airborne)** was also inactivated during this period, but was reactivated to remain at Fort Bragg, North Carolina since 1951, becoming the **XVIII Airborne Corps** in 1965.

The **82d Airborne Division** is the only airborne division to remain on active status since WW II, in the entire US Army. The **101st Airborne Division**, inactivated in 1945, returned for brief periods as a Training Division in the Organized Reserves, until reallocated back to the Active Component in 1956, and eventually into the current airmobile and air assault configurations while deployed in the Republic of Vietnam.

The primary thrust for retaining an airborne capability was through the US Army Organized Reserve Corps. In 1946 the **80th, 84th, 100th** and **108th Infantry Divisions** were reorganized as airborne divisions, to be activated that same year as the **80th, 100th** and **108th Airborne Divisions**, with the **84th Airborne Division** following in 1947. This was a short term, myopic solution, as all four divisions reverted to a non-airborne status in 1952.

The **11th Airborne Division** performed occupation duries in Germany from the early 1950s until inacti vation in 1958. The maneuver units assigned at that time were the**188th, 503d** and **511th Airborne Infantry Regiments** (assigned in **1950, 1951** and **1943** respectively). The **503d** had replaced the **187th**, which had deployed as a separate Regimental Combat Team to the Korean Conflict. In 1957, reorganized under the Pentomic System, the **11th Airborne Division** comprised of **1st Airborne Battle Groups, 187th** and **503d Infantry**, and the **2d Airborne Battle Groups, 502d, 504th** and **505th Infantry.** In 1958 the **2d AirborneBattle Groups of the 502d, 504th** and **505th Infantry** were inactivated with the **11th Airborne Division.** The **1st Airborne Battle Groups, 187th** and **503d Infantry** were assigned as the airborne combat arms elements of the **24th Infantry Division** un- til they were assigned to the **82d Airborne Division** at Fort Bragg, North Carolina in January/February 1959. The **2d Brigade, 24th Infantry** was not activated until 1963, and despite popular misconceptions, this was not the command and control for airborne elements of the **24th Infantry Division.** In December 1958, the **8th Infantry Division** assumed the former airborne missions of the **11th Airborne Division** and the **24th Infantry Division.** This responsibility was vested in the **1st Brigade (Abn)**, activated in Germany in 1963. The assigned elements, **1st Battalions** of the **504th** and **505th Airborne Infantry**, were respectively redesignated as the 1st and **2d Battalions, 509th Airborne Infantry.** Also in 1963, the **11th Airborne Division** was designated and activated as the **11th Air Assault Division** at Fort Benning, Georgia. So successful was the air assault concepts as demonstrated by the 11th Air Assault Division, resulting in the **1st Cavalry Division** being reconfigured for deployment to the Republic of Vietnam as the **1st Cavalry Division (Airmobile).** An extremely important organization, significantly contributing to the development of the air assault methodology, was the **10th Air Transport Brigade.** Constituted and activated in February 1963, the **10th Air Transport Brigade** commanded the **37th** and **44th Air Transport Battalions** and the **72d** and **516th Air Transport Companies.** These superb aviation units provided the precision flying that was necessary for the **11th Air Assault Division** to demonstrate air assault techniques. The **10th Air Transport Brigade** was inactivated concurrently with the **11th Air Assault Division** in 1965.

The **82d Airborne Division**, under direction of the **XVIII Airborne Corps**, was alerted and deployed to a crisis that had erupted in the Dominican Republic in 1965. All assets of the **XVIII Airborne Corps** and the **82d Airborne Division** returned to Fort Bragg, North Carolina during 1965-66.

Deploying in 1965, the **1st Cavalry Division (Airmobile),** provided an unprecedented success to the airmobile concept during combat operations in South East Asia. Their firepower and maneuverability were unequalled. The **1st Brigade** provided an initial airborne capability through the **1st** and **2d Battalions, 8th Cavalry,** and the **1st Battalion, 12th Cavalry**. The airmobile concept was deemed so successful for this type of terrain and environment, that the airborne capability was discontinued in 1966. The history, lineage and insignia of airborne armor, aviation and cavalry units will appear in Volume 4 of the Concise History Series - **<u>A Concise History of US Army Airborne Armor, Aviation and Cavalry Forces.</u>**

Also deploying early to South East Asia (as a Separate Brigade) in 1965, was the **1st Brigade, 101st Airborne Division,** commanded by **Col Joseph D. Mitchell** during August through September. **BG James S. Timothy** then assumed command from September 1965 until January 1966. For the following year, the brigade was commanded by **BG Willard Pearson**, who turned over the reins to **BG Salve H. Matheson** (the Iron Duke), in February 1967. **MG Olinto M. Barsanti**, brought the remainder of the **101st Airborne Division** to Vietnam in November 1967. Prior to the arrival of **MG Barsanti, BG Matheson** had declined the offer made by **GEN William C. Westmoreland,** Commander of **US Military Assistance Command Vietnam (MACV)**, to commit the **1st Brigade,** in an airborne operation. As history shows, the Sky Soldiers of the **173d Airborne Brigade** literally leapt at the chance, and provided **General Westmoreland** with his historic mass tactical airborne operation as the airborne phase of Operation **JUNCTION CITY**. The Iron Duke had participated with the **101st Airborne Division** in Bastogne and Normandy during WW II, and later with the **187th Regimental Combat Team** in Korea. **BG Matheson** relinquished command of the brigade to **COL** (later Brigadier General) **John (Rip) Collins**. The entire **101st Airborne Division** (with the exception of the Pathfinder Platoon), converted from an airborne status to become Airmoble during 1968-1969. The **101st Airborne Division (Airmobile)** redeployed to Fort Campbell, Kentucky in 1972.

In 1983, **LTG Jack V. Mackmull,** commanding **XVIII Airborne Corps**, committed the **82d Airborne Division** to the Caribbean island of Grenada during Operation **URGENT FURY**. This fast paced action was in response to the local government's plea for help in ridding Grenada of Cuban insurgents. US students attending a medical school on the island, had been placed in danger, thus solidifying the intervention of the United States. The operation was a tremendous success. **LTG Mackmull** had previously commanded the **101st Airborne Division,** and prior to that, the **US Army John F. Kennedy Center for Military Assistance**. In 1988, under command of (then) **MG Carl Stiner,** the **82d Airborne Division,** supported by assets of the **XVIII Airborne Corps,** provided a display of potential force and rapid strike capability in Honduras, in conjunction with exercise **GOLDEN PHEASANT.**

Two of the many outcomes of Operation **URGENT FURY** included the official approval finally being made to authorize the wearing of the Ranger Scroll SSI; also the wearing of stars to signify combat jumps on individual parachute badges. The tradition of wearing stars to signify the number of individual combat parachute assaults, had been in effect for almost half of a century, however the original request to wear the combat stars had been disapproved by **General George C. Marshall** as the Chief of Staff of the US Army during the second world war. Following Operation **URGENT FURY,** the **1st Special Operations Command,** Fort Bragg, North Carolina, during preparations to send representatives of the **Ranger Battalions,** who had participated in the airborne assault onto the island of Grenada, to the White House to receive decorations from **President Ronald W. Reagan,** the uniform insignia discrepancies were realized. Unless the Department of the Army approved the **Ranger Scroll** SSI and the wearing of combat stars, the **Ranger** representatives would have been wearing unauthorized insignia.The wearing of stars to signify individual combat jumps was approved retroactive to include World War II and all following hostilities, and the scroll orginally designed by **Brigadier General** (then Major) **William O. Derby,** finally became legal.

Chapter Three

First Airborne Army; Airborne Command and XVIII Airborne Corps

The US Army **Airborne Command** was activated at Fort Benning, Georgia from the **Provisional Parachute Group** in 1942, becoming the overall headquarters for the US Army Parachute Battalions, Glider Units, and the Parachute and Glider schools. The **Airborne Command** was redesignated as the **Airborne Center** in 1944, to be later disbanded in 1946. During the Second World War, the **Airborne Command** provided trained personnel for all five of the US Airborne Divisions, including 16 parachute infantry regiments, 12 glider infantry regiments, also supporting artillery, combat support and combat service support units.

Concurrently as the **Airborne Command** was redesignated as the **Airborne Center** in 1944, with total responsibility for all airborne forces within the Continental Unit States; the **First Allied Airborne Army** was activated from the redesignated **Combined Airborne Forces.** Organized at Ascot, England, this became the major planning headquarters for airborne forces committed to the European Theater of Operations (ETO). The commander of the **First Allied Airborne Army** was **Lieutenant General Lewis H. Brereton,** who had been tasked as a Major in 1918, by **General Jack Pershing,** to evaluate the feasibility of airborne forces.

The **First Airborne Task Force** was organized as a division-sized task force to spearhead Operation **DRAGON,** and was activated for three months during August through October 1944. Code named **Task Force RUGBY,** the **First Airborne Task Force,** headed by **General Robert T. Frederick** and his 1st Special Service Force (the Devils Brigade), landed in the Le Muy area of the South of France, blocking the advancing German army. Included with the **1st Special Service Force** in the **First Airborne Task Force,** was the **2d Independent Parachute Brigade** (UK); the **509th Combat Team** (comprising the **509th Parachute Infantry Battalion** and the **463d Parachute Field Artillery Battalion**); and the **517th Combat Team** (consisting of the **517th Parachute Infantry Regiment,** the **460th Parachute Field Artillery Battalion** and the **596th Airborne Engineer Company**). Additionally assigned were the **550th Airborne Infantry Battalion** and the **1st Battalion, 551st Parachute Infantry Regiment.** As units wore their own distinctive insignia and SSI, the reputed insignia of the **1st Airborne Task Force** was a circular cloth patch worn on the overseas cap, with a red glider and border on a white field (not verified).

In 1945, the **First Allied Airborne Army** relocated to Paris, where their foward Headquarters had been operating since 1944. Assigned elements of the **First Allied Airborne Army** included the **XVIII Corps (Airborne),** the **1st Airborne Corps** (UK) and the **IX Troop Carrier Command.** The **First Allied Allied Airborne Army** was responsible for the successful planning of Operation **MARKET GARDEN,** requiring the insertion and resupply of three airborne divisions into Holland in 1944. Other succesful operations planned and executed by the **First Allied Airborne Army,** took place at Einhoven and Nijmegen; also the resupply of the **101st Airborne Division** at Bastogne during the Battle of the Bulge; and the movement of two Airborne Divisions as part of Operation **VARSITY.** Later in 1945, the **First Allied Airborne Army** was disbanded, with the US element of that Headquarters assigned to the US **First Airborne Army.** Concurrent with it's activation, the **First Airborne Army** commenced occupation duties as the US Headquarters in the District of Berlin, Germany.

The **XVIII Corps (Airborne)** contributed significantly to the missions of the **First Allied Airborne Army,** preparing and writing the **MARKET** (airborne phase) of Operation **MARKET GARDEN,** and participated in Operation **BERLIN** (the withdrawal from Operation **MARKET GARDEN**), relocating to a forward HQ at Spernay, France. The Corps was deeply engaged in the severe fighting throughout the Reims-Sissoons-Suippes-

Mourmelon, and the Malmedy-Stavelot-Grand Menilareas; with Corps elements seizing the two key defensive areas along the Siegfried Line. Moving north into the Huertgen Forest, and two weeks later into Wesel, the **XVIII Corps (Airborne)** became involved in the airborne assault across the Rhine River. Later, attached to **First Army,** the **XVIII Corps (Airborne)** commanded the US **8th, 78th, 86th, and 97th Divisions.** Today, the **8th Infantry Division** remains in Germany, the **78th Division** was allocated to the USAR and converted to become the **78th Division (Training),** in New Jersey, and the **86th** and **97th** were redesignated to become the **86th** and **97th** Major **US Army Reserve Commands** (MUSARCS), in Forest Park IL, and Fort Meade MD, respectively. The lineage of both the **2d** and **3d Brigades** of the **82d Airborne Division** orginated from elements of the **78th Division,** while the roots of the **2d** and **3d Brigades** of the **101st Airborne Division,** came from the former **80th Airborne Division.** In 1987 the **86th** and **97th Army Reserve Command**s, were designated as the SOF MUSARCS, to which all USAR Special Operations Forces are assigned in the **First** and **Fourth Continental US Army** (CONUSA) areas. The **120th** and **90th MUSARCs** were designated as the SOF MUSARCs for **Second** and **Fifth Armies** respectively, with the **351st Civil Affairs Command** already in this capacity for **Sixth US Army.**

The **II Armored Corps** was redesignated as the **XVIII Corps** at Camp Bowie, Texas in 1943. Coming from an armor heritage, the shoulder sleeve insignia (SSI) that was initially, (prematurely and not authorized) manufactured, followed the traditional triangular design of the tanker's *'pyramid of power',* representing the infantry, artllery and cavalry origins of the armored forces. The Roman Numerals XVIII were included in the apex of the SSI. In February 1944, a diamond shaped SSI in the traditional US Corps colors of blue and white, with the head of a dragon looking directly to the left, was authorized, manufactured and worn. Deploying to Ogbourne St George in England in August 1944, the **XVIII Corps** was reorganized and redesignated as **the XVIII Corps (Airborne),** and assigned to the **First Allied Airborne Army.** The diamond shaped SSI was rotated ninety degrees counter-clockwise, (with the dragon's head now looking symbolically down from the skies), and the blue and white airborne tab added, resulting in the SSI that contionues to be proudly worn at Fort Bragg today. The **XVIII Corps (Airborne)** was inactivated from 1945 until 1951, to be later redesignated and concurrently activated at Fort Bragg as the **XVIII Airborne Corps** in 1965.

Although not specifically designated as an Airborne Command, the **1st Corps Support Command (1st COSCOM),** is included for a number of reasons. The **1st COSCOM,** at Fort Bragg, provides the total combat service support for the **XVIII Airborne Corps.** Numbering only 6,500 personnel under Command of a Colonel in peacetime; this expands to more than 25,000 assigned personnel (active, ARNG and USAR), when transitioning to a wartime configuration. Under a wartime footing, the **1st Corps Support Command** is commanded by a Major General. While commanded by **Colonel William J. Richardson Jr** (1980-84), six airborne positions were authorized in **HHC, 1st COSCOM,** justified through command of the two largest airborne quartermaster rigger companies in the active component inventory - the **600th Quartermaster Company (Air Equipment R-S),** and the **612th Quartermaster Company (Air Delivery).** This was expanded under the consecutive commands of **Colonels Dane Starling** and **George B. Dibble,** to more than 30 airborne positions. **BG (P) Starling** became the Director or Logistics and Security Assistance for the **US Central Command** in June 1989.

<u>Commanders, XVIII Airborne Corps</u>

John W. LEONARD	1951-1952	John L. THROCKMORTON	1967
Thomas F. HICKEY	1952-1953	Robert H. YORK	1967-1968
Joseph P. CLELAND	1953-1955	John L. TOLSON	1968-1971
Ridgley GAITHER	1955	John H. HAY Jr	1971-1973
Paul D. ADAMS	1955-1957	Richard J. SEITZ	1973-1975
Robert F. SINK	1957-1960	Henry E. EMERSON	1975-1977
Thomas J. H. TRAPNELL	1960-1961	Volney E. WARNER	1977-1979
Hamilton H. HOWZE	1961-1963	Thomas H. TACKABERRY	1979-1981
Wm C. WESTMORELAND	1963-1965	Jack V. MACKMULL	1981-1984
John BOWEN	1964-1965	James J. LINDSAY	1984-1986
Bruce PALMER	1965-1967	John W. FOSS	1986-1988

LTG Carl W. Stiner, 1988 to Present

First Allied Airborne Army

**First Allied Airborne
Army SSI 1944-45**

**First US Airborne Army
(SSI Variations 1945)**

1944   Formed from the redesignated **Combined Airborne Forces.**

Activated at Ascot, England, with a forward Command Post located near Paris, France.

Deployed elements to France and directed **Operation MARKET GARDEN.**

Provided support to the **101st Airborne Division** at Bastogne, during the Battle of the Bulge.

Coordinated the transportation of the **17th Airborne Division** from the Continental United States (CONUS), to the European Theater of Operations (ETO).

1945   **HQ, First Allied Airborne Army** relocated to forward Command Post Headquarters, near Paris, France.

Planned and executed **Operation VARSITY.**

Disbanded by direction of the **Supreme Allied Headquarters.**

Redesignated as the **First US Airborne Army.**

Relocated to Berlin as **HQ, US Sector of Berlin,** Germany.

Inactivated at Berlin, Germany.

US Army Airborne Command

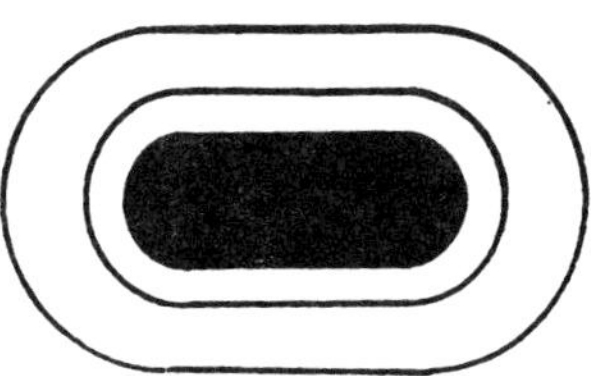

USA Airborne Cmd Oval

US A   Airborne Cmd SSI

1941	Constituted in the Regular Army as **HQ, Provisional Parachute Group.** Activated at Fort Benning, Georgia.
1942	Reorganized and redesignated as the **Airborne Command.** Relocated to Fort Bragg, North Carolina, (with the **Airborne School** remaining at Fort Benning, Georgia).
1944	Relocated to Fort Benning, Georgia. Redesignated as **The Airborne Center.**
1946	Inactivated and discontinued at Fort Benning, Georgia.

US Army Parachute Badge

US Army Glider Badge

XVIII Airborne Corps

XVIII Abn Corps
DUI 1987

XVIII Abn Corps
Flash and Oval

XVIII Abn Corps
(XVIII Corps (Abn)
1944

1943	Constituted from the **II Armored Corps.** Redesignated as **HHC, XVIII Corps.** Activated at the Presidio of Monterey, California. Relocated to Camp Bowie, Texas.
1944	Relocated to Fort Dupont, Delaware. Deployed to England in the ETO of World War II.

1944   World War II Campaign Participation included the **Rhineland, Ardennes-Alsace** and **Central Europe.**

Reorganized and redesignated as **HHC, XVIII Corps (Airborne)**
Assigned to the **First Allied Airborne Army.**

Provided logistical and technical planning expertise during Operation **MARKET GARDEN.**

Forward Headquarters located at Spernay, France.
XVIII Corps (Airborne) relocated to Werbonnet, Belgium.

1945   Relocated to the Huertgen Forest, Germany.

Relocated to Spernay, France, to prepare and coordinate the Rhine Crossing operations of the **6th** (British) **Airborne Division** and the **17th Airborne Division**

Assigned to **First Army**, with operational command of the **8th, 78th, 86th** and **97th Infantry Divisions**, and the **13th Armored Division.**

Attached to the **British Second Army**, with command of the British **6th Airborne Division;**

the US **8th Infantry Division** and the **82d Airborne Division.**

Redeployed to CONUS.

1951	Activated at Fort Bragg, North Carolina. Assigned to the **US Army Strike Command.**
1965	Reorganized and redesignated as **HQ, XVIII Airborne Corps.** **XVIII Airborne Corps** concurrently constituted and activated at Fort Bragg, North Carolina. Deployed and commanded all US Military Forces employed in the Dominican Republic crisis.
1966	Redeployed last elements to Fort Bragg, North Carolina.
1979	Assigned as the Army Component HQ of the **US Rapid Deployment Joint Task Force (RDJTF).**
1981	Assigned to **Third US Army** in support of the **US Central Command.**
1983	Commanded US Army elements deployed to Grenada.
1988	Participated in Operation **GOLDEN PHEASANT** in Honduras.

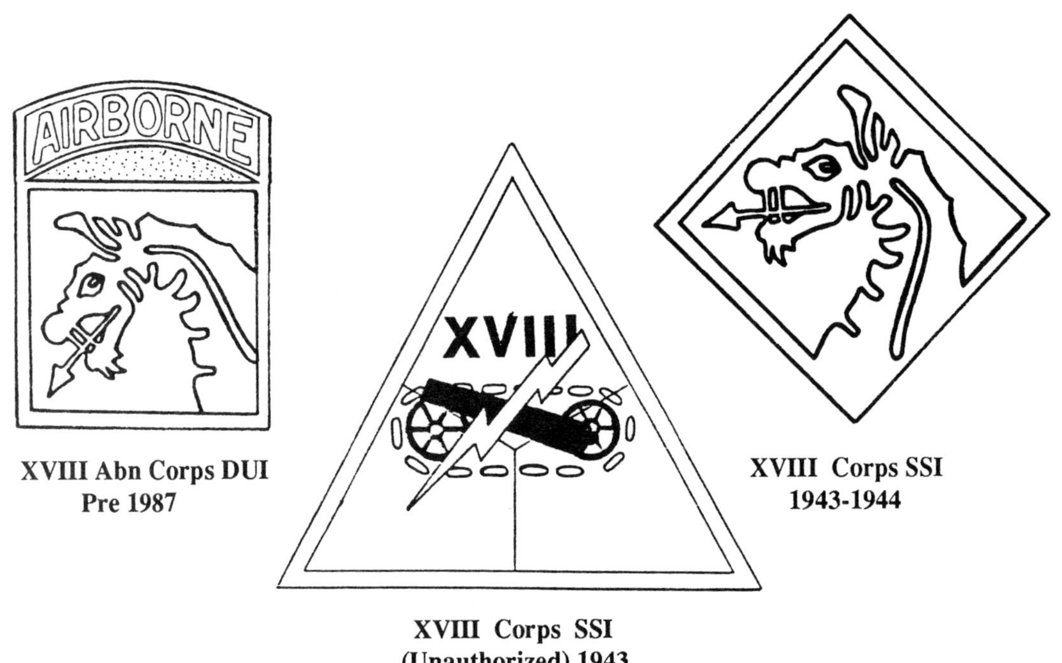

XVIII Abn Corps DUI
Pre 1987

XVIII Corps SSI
1943-1944

XVIII Corps SSI
(Unauthorized) 1943

1ST CORPS SUPPORT COMMAND

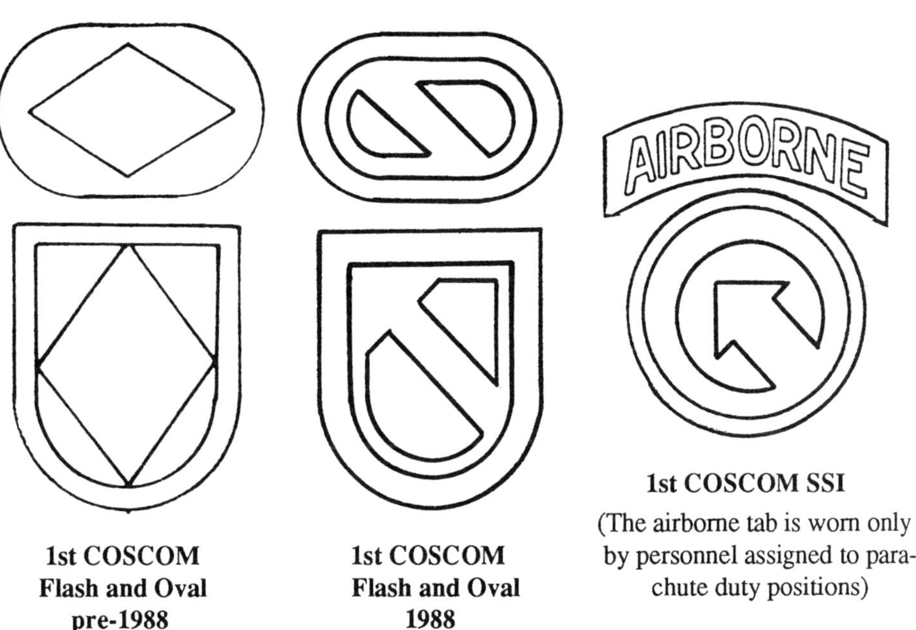

1st COSCOM
Flash and Oval
pre-1988

1st COSCOM
Flash and Oval
1988

1st COSCOM SSI
(The airborne tab is worn only
by personnel assigned to parachute duty positions)

1950	Constituted in the Regular Army as **HQ, 1st Logistical Command.** Assigned to **Third US Army.** Activated at Fort McPherson, Georgia.
1961	**HQ Company**, (constituted 1952 in the Regular Army), activated at Fort Bragg, North Carolina). Disbanded at Fort Bragg, North Carolina.

1961

HQ, 1st Logistical Command reorganized and redesignated as **HHC, 1st Logistical Cnd.**

Deployed to establish a Logistical Headquarters in France during the Berlin Crisis.

1962

Redeployed to Fort Hood, Texas
Assigned to **Fourth US Army.**

Reorganized and redesignated as **HHD, 1st Logistical Command.**

1965

Deployed to the Republic of Vietnam.
Assigned to **US Army Pacific.**

Vietnam Campaign Participation included the **Defensive; Counteroffensive; Counteroffensive Phases II, III, IV, V, VI and VII; Tet Counteroffensive; Tet 69/Counteroffensive; Summer-Fall 1969; Winter-Spring 1970;** and the **Sanctuary Counteroffensive.**

1966

Meritorious Unit Commendation, with Streamer embroidered **VIETNAM 1965**, awarded to **HHD, 1st Logistical Command.**

| 1967 | **Meritorious Unit Commendation**, with Streamer embroidered **VIETNAM 1966**, awarded to **HHD, 1st Logistical Command.** |

| 1968 | **Meritorious Unit Commendation**, with Streamer **embroidered VIETNAM 1967-1968**, awarded to **HHD, 1st Logistical Command.** |

| 1970 | **Meritorious Unit Commendation,** with Streamer embroidered **VIETNAM 1969-1970**, awarded to **HHD, 1st Logistical Command.** |

Redeployed to Fort Lee, Virginia.
Received assignments of personnel from the inactivated **22d Field Army Support Command.**

1972

Reorganized and redesignated as **HHC and Special Troops, 1st Field Army Support Cmd**
Relocated to Fort Bragg, North Carolina.
Assigned to **XVIII Airborne Corps,** under **First US Army.**
Reorganized and redesignated as **HHC, 1st Corps Support Command (1st COSCOM).**

1980   Redesignated as **HHC, 1st Support Command (1st SUPCOM).**

1982   Redesignated as **HHC, 1st Corps Support Command (1st COSCOM).**

1st COSCOM DUI

(**NOTE:** The Airborne Tab worn over the **1st COSCOM** SSI, is authorized for personnel assigned to duty parachute positions in **HHC, 1st COSCOM,** and personnel assigned to the **600th** and **612th Quartermaster Companies**). TheDUIs, airborne ovals and beret flashes of the airborne quartermaster units will be included in the **Concise History of US Army Airborne Combat Service Support.**

Chapter Four

US Army Airborne Divisions

The first of the US Army Airborne Divisions, were the **82d** (All American), and the **101st** (Screaming Eagles) **Airborne Divisions**; formerly the **82d** and **101st Infantry Divisions**. Both were redesignated as Airborne Divisions and activated from the Organized Reserves on 15 August 1942. As US involvement in the Second World War became more imminent, the **11th Airborne** (Angels) **Division,** was activated at Camp Mackall, North Carolina on 25 February 1943, followed by the **17th Airborne** (Golden Talon - or Thunder from Heaven) **Division** at Camp Mackall, on 15 April 1943. The **13th Airborne Division** was activated in August 1943, at Fort Bragg, North Carolina The **15th Airborne Division**, although constituted with units designated for assignment, was never activated.

The **11th Airborne Division** fought valiantly in the Pacific Theater where, during three campaigns, they were awarded the **US Presidential Unit Citation (Army)** and the **Philippine Presidential Unit Citation. MG Joseph M. Swing,** (who gave them the nickname 'The Angels"), was the first commander of the **11th Airborne Division. MG Swing** had previously commanded the **1st Cavalry Division Artillery.** The Angels deployed to the Pacific Theater where their gallant actions are legend. In 1944 when 250 Japanese paratroopers assaulted onto the San Pablo airstrip, US paratroopers fought a fierce adversary, but totally annihilated the Japanese paratroopers. Continuing on, more than 5,700 enemy soldiers were killed by the Division. After a short respite, the Angels performed an amphibious assault onto Nasugbu on the southwestern coast of Luzon. The next month the **511th Parachute Infantry** conducted an airborne assault near the Manila Hotel Annex. After Manila, Imus and Nasugbu, the Division moved to Bacoor and the Genko Line, where they linked with the **1st Cavalry Division**. The Luzon campaign was completed with the capture of Nichols Field and Fort McKinley. In a combined air and sea assault, the **11th Airborne Division** liberated the prison camp at Los Banos. The Division was tasked to police the 55,000 square mile Batangas Province, south of Manila. Following WW II, the Angels performed occupation duty in the Sendai-Fukufhima area, 200 miles north of Tokyo, Japan Next followed an assignment to Germany. Fron 1963 through 1965, they were redesignated as the **11th Air Assault Division,** and activated at Fort Benning, Georgia paving the way to later highly succussful airmobile operational concepts.

The **13th Airborne Division** was activated on Friday the 13th of August, 1943. The Black Cat nickname, often associated with the **13th Airborne Division**, is really attributed to the **13th Armored Division**. The **13th Airborne Division** was assigned to the the **First Allied Airborne Army** in the ETO, but never committed to combat as a Division. Although alerted for participation in Operations **VARSITY**, the Division was withdrawn prior to implementation. The Division was scheduled for Operation **CHOKER II**, but this operation was cancelled as was Operation **EFFECTIVE** in 1945. The Division is credited with one campaign during their assignment to the ETO. **PFC Melvin E. Biddle (517th Parachute Infantry)**, was awarded the Congressional Medal of Honor for actions in Belgium. **Major General George W. Griner** commanded the **13th Airborne Division** from activation until November 1943. His replacement was **Major General Elbridge G. Chapman** whose command continued through inactivation in February 1946 at Fort Bragg, North Carolina, was a recipient of the Distinguished Service Cross and the Silver Star with Oak Leaf Cluster during the First World War.

From April 1943 until inactivation, the **17th Airborne Division** was commanded by **Major General William M. Miley** (the first commander of the **501st Parachute Battalion** in 1940). Followingr his assignment to the **501st Parachute Battalion, MG Miley** had served as the Commander, 1st Airborne Infantry Brigade, and Assistant Division Commander, **82d Airborne Division.**

During the Battle of the Bulge, the **17th Airborne Division** participated in spectacular night transport landings in the Rheims area. The Golden Talon later provided security along the Meusse River during the Ardennes Campaign, later relieving the **11th Armored Division** to provide defensive forces between the **101st Airborne** and

87th Infantry Divisions, south of Bastogne. Attacking through the icy blizzard, the **17th** took Cetturu, Bouitet, Steinbach and Limerle invading into Germany near Wiltz. Successively, the Division advanced through Clerveaux, Luxembourg, to participate in the airborne assault northeast of Wesel, Germany. The big push had commenced, continuing through Dorsten, Haltern, Dulman, Appelhalsen, and on into Munster. Following came the battle of the Ruhr Pocket, where the Golden Talon relieved the **79th Division** along the Rhine-Herne Canal. Crossing the Canal, the Division established the bridgehead into Essen, Muleim, Duisberg and Werden. Postumous Congressional Medals of Honor were awarded to **T/Sgt Clinton M. Hedrick, PFC Stuart S. Stryker** and **PVT George J. Peters**. Distinguished Service Crosses were awarded to **PFCs Herman L. Longerbeam** and **Thomas Manuel** of the **194th Glider Infantry Regiment; PFCs Dante T. Toneguzzo** and **J. C. Upton Jr** of the **507th Parachute Infantry Regiment;** and **Corporal Samuel D. Strain** of the **155th Airborne Anti-aircraft Artillery Battalion.**

The **82d Infantry Division** was reactivated on 25 March 1942 at Camp Claiborne, Louisiana, under the command of **Major General Omar N. Bradley.** Five months later they were redesignated as the **82d Airborne Division**, under command of **Major General Matthew B. Ridgeway.** During six campaigns in the ETO, the All Americans participated in four airborne assaults behind enemy lines at Gela, Sicily, at the Salerno beachhead, at Normandy, and in Holland. The **505th Parachute Infantry Regiment** was the only regiment to participate in all four operations. An element of the Division, the **2d Battalion, 509th Parachute Infantry Regiment** made an amphibious assault at Anzio on 23 January 1944. On 8 February, **CPL Paul B. Huff** became the first paratrooper in the US Army to be awarded the Congressional Medal of Honor during that action. (He later earned a star for his Combat Infantryman Badge while assigned to the **1st Brigade, 101st Airborne Division,** in the Republic of Vietnam). Later the **82d Airborne Division** thwarted **General Von Rundstedt's** northern salient during the Battle of the Bulge. **LTC Emory Pike** and **CPL Alvin C. York** were awarded the Congressional Medals of Honor during WW I with the **82d Division.** During WW II the Nation's highest award for valor was presented to **1SG Leonard Funk, PFC Charles N. DeGlopper** and (postumously) to **PVT John R. Towle.** Additional valor awards presented within the ranks of the **82d** during WW II included 79 Distinguished Service Crosses and 894 Silver Stars.

The nickname **'America's Guard of Honor'** was given to the All Americans during the post-war occupation of Berlin. In 1964, the Division was assigned to the Army **STRIKE COMMAND**, providing the ready spearhead of the US Army, prepared to deploy to any worldwide situation. Exactly 22 years to the day, following the **82d Airborne Division's** departure for the ETO on 29 April 1943, the Division was committed to Operation **POWER PACK**, to keep the peace in the revolt-torn Dominican Republic, in 1965, with the last elements returning to Fort Bragg, North Carolina in 1966.

Internally, within the Continental United States, during 1967-1968, brigade sized elements of the **82d Airborne Division** were deployed to assist in civil disturbances in Detroit, Michigan and twice to Washington, DC.

The **3d Brigade, 82d Airborne Division** was deployed to the Republic of Vietnam, initially attached to the **101st Airborne Division**, then relocated to defend Saigon following the Tet Offensive of 1968. The **3d Brigade** participated in six campaigns during their assigment to South East Asia. The Republic of Vietnam **Cross of Gallantry with Palm**, and the **Civic Action Honor Medal First Class**, were awarded to the **3d Brigade.** During the absence of the **3d Brigade** from Fort Bragg, the **4th Brigade, 82d Airborne Division** was activated to continue a full airborne division in readiness to support the US Army **STRIKE COMMAND.** In December 1983, the **82d Airborne Division** was again alerted and rapidly deployed to the Caribbean Island of Grenada at the request of the legal government of that country. Under command of the **XVIII Airborne Corps**, the Division assisted in the routing of Cuban insurgents, and the safeguarding of US medical students. The US **Armed Forces Expedionary Streamer** was awarded to the **82d Airborne Division.**

Major General James M. (Slim Jim) **Gavin** followed **MG Ridgeway** as the wartime commander of the **82d Airborne Division.** Subsequent commanders have included **Brigadier Generals William P. Branham, James Erwin** and **Ridgely Gaither** and **Major Generals Clovis E. Byers, Williston B. Palmer, Thomas P. Hickey, Charles D. W. Canham, Francis W. Farrell, John W. Bowen, Hamilton H. Howze, John L. Throckmorton, Robert H. York, Joe S. Lawrie, Richard J. Seitz, John R. Deane, George S. Blanchard, Frederick J. Kroesen, Thomas H. Tackaberry, Roscoe Robinson Jr, Guy S. Meloy, James J. Lindsay, Edward. L. Trobaugh, Bobby B. Porter, John Foss, Carl W. Stiner** and **James H. Johnson Jr.** Generals

Bowen, Throckmorton, York, Seitz, Tackaberry, Lindsay, Foss and **Stiner** continued in their airborne assignments to command the **XVIII Airborne Corps.** At the time of this writing, **General Lindsay** commands the **US Special Operations Command** and **LTG Foss** is the Deputy Chief of Staff for Operations (DCSOPS) of the US Army. **LTG Stiner**, former commander of the **Joint Special Operations Command** prior to command of the **82d Airborne Division**, presently commands the **XVIII Airborne Corps.**

The **101st Airborne Division**, (formerly the **101st Infantry Division**), was reorganized and redesignated as an Airborne Division from cadre of the **82d Airborne Division** in August 1942 Following intensive training at Fort Brtagg, North Carolina and in Tennessee, the Screaming Eagles deployed to the ETO in September 1943. On June 6th, 1944, the **101st Airborne Division** conducted an airborne assault near Utah Beach, Normandy, France. The Division swung into the attack after rallying the troops, capturing Pouppeville, Vierville, St Come Du Mont and Carentan. Returning to England, the Screaming Eagles regrouped, prepared, and executed another airborne assault (into Holland) as part of Operation **MARKET GARDEN**, capturing Veghel, and the bridges at Veghel, Oedenrode and Zon. Moving South, the Division captured Eindhoven. After several ownerships by both sides, the town of Opheusden was secured before the Division returned to Mourmelon, France. Prior to Christmas 1944, the **101st Airborne Division** moved to defend the city of Bastogne, where they became surrounded by enemy forces. It was during this encirclement that **MG Anthony C. McCauliffe**, commanding the **101st Airborne Division,** issued his historic response of 'Nuts!' to the German invitation to surrender. The surrounding forces were broken by the US **4th Armored Division**, allowing the Screaming Eagles to take the offensive. The cities of Neville and Bourcy fell, reducing the Bulge. The Division then cleaned the Ruhr Pocket before continuing East to Berchtesgaden and the cessation of hostilities. The Division had fought in four campaigns, with a loss of more than nine thousand casualties. **Two Presidential Unit Citations (Army)**, the **French** and **Belgium Croix des Guerre**, the **Belgian Fourragere** and the **Netherlands Oramge Lanyard** were awarded to the 101st Airborne Division.

Following the Second World War in 1946, the United States beefed-up army airborne capabilities by reorganizing and redesignating in the Organized Reserves, the **80th, 84th, 100th** and **108th Infantry Divisions** as the **80th, 84th, 100th** and **108th** (Golden Griffin) **Airborne Divisions.** This was a short term fix, that was reversed in 1952 when these divisions were redesignated as reserve Training Divisions. Only the **3d Brigade, 108th Airborne Division (Training)**, does not have an airborne lineage.

In 1965 the **1st Brigade, 101st Airborne Division** was deployed to the Republic of Vietnam, with the remainder of the Division following from Fort Campbell, Kentucky, in 1967. The **1st Brigade** participated in 15 campaigns, with the remainder of the Division participated in twelve. **SGM Paul B. Huff,** the first US Army paratrooper to be awarded the Congressional Medal of Honor, had volunteered for deployment, and served as the Sergeant Major of the **1st Brigade.** Two **Presidential Unit Citations (Army)**, the French and Belgian **Croix des Guerre**, Belgian **Fourragere** and the Netherlands **Orange Lanyard** were awarded to the **101st Airborne Division** for actions during World War II. Four Republic of Vietnam **Crosses of Gallantry with Palm**, and the **Civic Action Honor Medal First Class** were awarded to elements of the **101st Airborne Division** for actions in Vietnam.

While deployed in Vietnam, by July 1969, the **101st Airborne Division** (less the Pathfinder platoon), was converted to an Airmobile configuration, still retaining Airborne as part of their title. Later, the Screaming Eagles were redesignated as the **101st Airborne Division (Air Assault).**

HHC, 11th Airborne Division

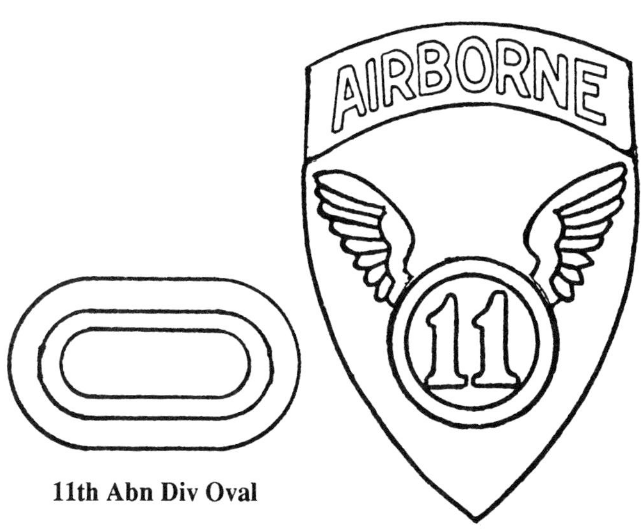

11th Abn Div Oval

11th Airborne Div SSI

1942	Constituted in the AUS as **HQ, 11th Airborne Division.**
1943	Activated at Camp Mackall, North Carolina. Assigned to the US **Airborne Center.** Embarked for New Guinea. Assigned to the Pacific Theater of Operations World War II Campaign Participation included **New Guinea, Leyte** and **Luzon** (with arrowhead).
1945	**Presidential Unit Citation (Army).** with Streamer embroidered **MANILA**, awarded to **HQ, 11th Airborne Division.**
1948	Allotted to the Regular Army.
1950	**Philippine Presidential Unit Citation,** with Streamer embroidered **17 OCTOBER 1944 TO 4 JULY 1945,** awarded to the **11th Airborne Division.**
1957	Reorganized and redesignated as **HHC, Command and Contol Bn, 11th Airborne Division.**
1958	Inactivated in Germany.
1963	Redesignated as the **11th Air Assault Division.** Activated at Fort Benning, Georgia.
1965	Inactivated at Fort Benning, Georgia.
1972	Redesignated as **HHC, 11th Airborne Division.**

HHC, 1st Brigade 11th Airborne Division

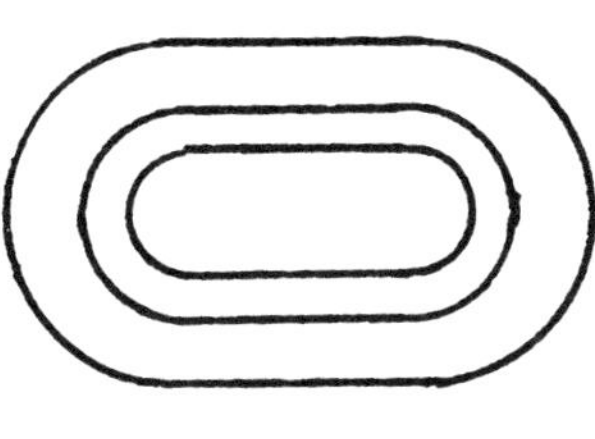

11th Abn Div Oval

11th Airborne Div SSI

1942	Constituted in the AUS as **HQ Company, 11th Airborne Division.**
1943	Activated at Camp Mackall, North Carolina.
	World War II Campaign Participation included **New Guinea, Leyte** and **Luzon** (with arrow head).
	Presidential Unit Citation (Army), with Streamer embroidered **MANILA** awarded to the **11th Airborne Division.**
1948	Allotted to the Regular Army.
1950	**Philippine Presidential Unit Citation,** with Streamer embroidered **17 OCTOBER 1944 TO 4 JULY 1945** awarded to the **11th Airborne Division.**
1957	Reorganized and redesignated as **HHC, Command and Control Battalion, 11th Airborne Division.**
1958	Inactivated in Germany.
1963	Redesignated as **HHC, 1st Brigade, 11th Air Assault Division.** Activated at Fort Benning, Georgia,
1965	Inactivated at Fort Benning, Georgia.
1972	Redesignated as **HHC, 1st Brigade, 11th Airborne Division.**

HHC, 2d Brigade, 11th Airborne Division

1963   Constituted in the Regular Army as **HHC, 2d Brigade, 11th Air Assault Division.** Activated at Fort Benning, Georgia.

1965   Inactivated at Fort Benning, Georgia.

1972   Redesignated as **HHC, 2d Brigade, 11th Airborne Division**

HHC, 3d Brigade, 11th Airborne Division

1964   Constituted in the Regular Army as **HHC, 3d Brigade, 11th Air Assault Division.** Activated at Fort Benning, Georgia.

1965   Inactivated at Fort Benning, Georgia.

1972   Redesignated as **HHC, 3d Brigade, 11th Airborne Division.**

11th Air Assault Div Badge

11th Air Assault Div SSI

HHC, 13th Airborne Division

13th Airborne Div SSI

1942	Constituted in the AUS as **HHC, 13th Airborne Division.**
1943	Activated at Fort Benning, Georgia
1944	Relocated and reassigned to the **Airborne Command,** Camp Mackall, North Carolina. Assigned to the **Airborne Center.**
1945	Deployed to the ETO. Assigned to the **First Allied Airborne Army.**
	World War II Campaign Participation included **Central Europe.**
	Redeployed to CONUS, pending reassignment to the Pacific Theater.
1946	Inactivated.

HHC, 17th Airborne Division

17th Airborne Div SSI

1942	Constituted in the AUS as **HHC, 17th Airborne Division.**
1943	Activated at Camp Mackall, North Carolina. Assigned to the **US Airborne Command.**
1944	Deployed to the ETO. World War II Campaign Participation included the **Rhineland, Ardennes-Alsace** and **Central Europe** (with arrowhead).
1945	Assigned to the **First Allied Airborne Army.**
1945	Inactivated at Camp Myles Standish, Massachusetts.
1948	Allotted to the Regular Army. Activated at Camp Pickett, Virginia.
1949	Inactivated at Camp Pickett, Virginia.

HQ, 80th Airborne Division

80th Div (Tng) DUI 1970   **80th Abn Div SSI**

1917	Constituted in the National Army as **HQ, 80th Division.** Organized at Camp Lee, Virginia. World War I Campaign Participation included the **Somme Offensive** and the Meuse-Argonne.
1919	Demobilized at Camp Lee, Virginia.
1921	Reconstituted in the Organized Reserves as **HQ, 80th Division.** Organized at Richmond, Virginia.
1942	Redesignated as **Division HQ, 80th Division.** Ordered into Active Military Service. Reorganized at Camp Forrest, Tennessee. Redesignated as **HQ, 80th Infantry Division.** World War II Campaign Participation included **Northern France** the **Rhineland, Ardennes-Alsace** and **Central Europe.**
1946	Inactivated at Camp Kilmer, New Jersey. Redesignated as **HQ, 80th Airborne Division.** Allotted to the Organized Reserves, and assigned to **Second Army** Activated at Richmond, Virginia.
1952	Reorganized and redesignated as **HQ, 80th Infantry Division.**
1959	Reorganized and redesignated as **HHC, 80th Division (Training).**
1966	Relieved from assignment to the **Second US Army.** Assigned to **First US Army.**

NOTE: The shown DUI of the **80th Division (Training)** and Non Color Bearing Units (NCBU) was authorized in May 1970, with first samples approved on 23 October 1970.

HHD, 1st Brigade, 80th Division (Training)
(HQ Company, 80th Airborne Division)

**80th Div (Tng) DUI
1970**

80th Abn Div SSI

1917	Constituted in the National Army as **HQ Troop, 80th Division**, organized at Camp Lee, Va.
	World War II Campaign Participation included the **Somme-Offensive**, andthe**Meusse-Ar gonne**
1919	Demobilized at Camp Lee, Virginia.
1921	Reconstituted in the Organized Reserves as **HQ Company, 80th Division..** Organized at Richmond, Virginia.
1942	Reorganized and redesignated as **HQ and Military Police Company** (less the M P Platoon)
	Ordered into Active Military Service, reorganized at Camp Forrest, Tennessee. Redesignated as **HQ Company, 80th Infantry Division.**
	World War II Campaigns included **N France, Rhineland, Ardennes- Alsace** and **Cent Europe.**
1946	Inactivated at Camp Kilmer, New Jersey. Redesignated as **HQ Company, 80th Airborne Division.** Allotted to the Organized Reserves, activated at Richmond, Virginia.
1949	Disbanded at Richmond, Virginia
1952	Reorganized and redesignated as **HQ Company, 80th Infantry Division.**
1967	Reconstituted in the Army Reserve as **HHD, 1st Brigade, 80th Division (Training).**
1968	Activated at Alexandria, Virginia.

HHD, 2d Brigade, 80th Division (Training)
(905th Glider Field Artillery Battalion)

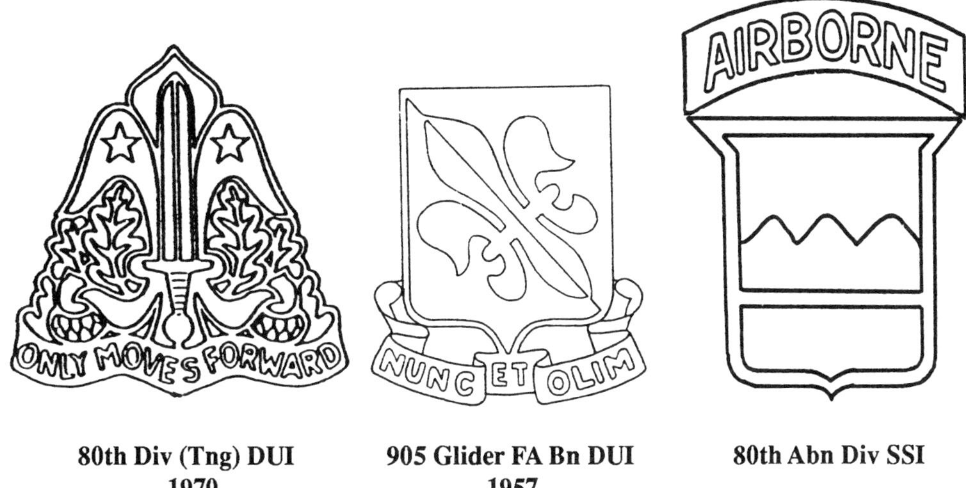

| 80th Div (Tng) DUI 1970 | 905 Glider FA Bn DUI 1957 | 80th Abn Div SSI |

1917
Constituted in the National Army as the **305th Ammunition Train.**
Assigned to the **80th Division.**
Organized at Camp Lee, Virginia.
World War I Campaign Participation was the **Meuse-Argonne.**

1919
Demobilized at Camp Dix, New Jersey.

1936
Reorganized in the Organized Reserves; concurrently consolidated with the **305th Ammunition Train** (organized in December 1921 in the Organized Reserves with Headquarters in Washington, DC), with the consolidated unit designated as the **305th Ammunition Train,** an element of the **80th Division.**

1942
Converted and redesignated as the **905th Field Artillery Battalion, 80th Division.**
Ordered into Active Military Service, reorganized at Camp Forrest, Tennessee.
World War II Campaign Participation included **Northern France, Rhineland, Ardennes-Alsace** and **Central Europe.**

1946
Inactivated at Camp Kilmer, New Jersey, allotted to the Organized Reserves.
Redesignated as the **905th Glider Field Artillery Battalion, 80th Airborne Division.**

1947
Activated at Bristol, Virginia.

1950
Redesignated as the **905th Field Artillery Battlion.**

1959
Disbanded at Bristol, Virginia.

1967
HHB, 905th F A Bn reconstituted in the Army Reserve as **HHD, 2d Bde, 80th Div (Tng).**

1968
Activated at Salem, Virginia.

HHC, 3d Brigade,
80th Division (Training)
(305th Airborne Engineer Battalion)

**80th Div (Tng) DUI
1970**

305th Abn Engr Bn DUI

80th Abn Div SSI

1917	Constituted in the National Army as the **305th Engineers**. Assigned to the **80th Division**. Organized at Camp Lee, Virginia.

1917   Constituted in the National Army as the **305th Engineers**.
Assigned to the **80th Division**.
Organized at Camp Lee, Virginia.

World War II Campaign Participation included the **Somme Offensive**, the **Meuse-Argonne** and **Picardy 1918.**

1919   Demobilized at Camp Dix, New Jersey.

1921   Reconstituted in the Organized Reserve as the **305th Engineers**.
Assigned to the **80th Division**.
Organized with Headquarters at Richmond, Virginia.

1942   Redesignated (less 2d Battalion), as the **305th Engineer Battalion**.
(The 2d Battalion hereafter follows a separate lineage).

Ordered into Active Military Service.
Reorganized at Camp Forrest, Tennessee.
Redesignated as the **305th Engineer Combat Battalion**.

World War II Campaign Participation included **Northern France, Rhineland, Ardennes-Alsace** and **Central Europe.**

1946   Inactivated at Camp Dix, New Jersey.
Redesignated as the **305th Airborne Engineer Battalion**.
Allotted to the Organized Reserves.

Assigned to the **80th Airborne Division.**

1947	Activated at Richmond, Virginia.
1952	Redesignated as the **305th Engineer Combat Battalion.** Assigned to the **80th Infantry Division.**
1953	Redesignated as the **305th Engineer Battalion.**
1954	Activated at Richmond, Virginia.
1956	Activated with Headquarters at Abington, Virginia.
1959	Disbanded (less Companies A and B), at Abington, Virginia. (Companies A and B hereafter follow a separate lineage).
1967	**HHSC, 305th Engineer Battalion** reconstituted in the Army Reserve. Reorganized and redesignated as **HHD, 3d Brigade, 80th Division (Training).**
1968	Activated at Richmond, Virginia.
1971	Reorganized and redesignated as **HHC, 3d Brigade, 80th Division (Training**
1973	Inactivated at Richmond, Virgnia.

First US Army SSI

HHD, 4th Brigade, 80th Division (Training)
(780th Airborne Ordnance Maintenance Co)

80th Div (Tng) DUI
1970

80th Abn Div SSI

1917   Constituted in the National Army as the **305th Supply Train.**
Assigned to the **80th Division.**

1918   Organized at Camp Lee, Virginia.

World War I Campaign Participation included **Meuse-Argonne.**

1919   Demobilized at Camp Dix, New Jersey.

1936   Reconstituted in the Organized Reserves and concurrently consolidated with the **405th Quartermaster Regiment** (organized in 1921 in the Organized Reserves, with Headquarters at Richmond, Virginia, as the **80th Division Train, Quartermaster Corps;** redesignated in 1925 as the **80th Division Quartermaster Train;** redesignated in 1936 as the **405th Quartermaster Regiment**), with the consolidated unit designated as the **405th Quartermaster Regiment.**

Assigned to the **80th Division.**

1942   Redesignated as the **405th Quartermaster Battalion.**

Ordered into Active Military Service.
Reorganized at Camp Forrest, Tennessee.

The **Ordnance Maintenance Platoon** reorganized and redesignated as the **780th Ordnance Light Maintenance Company.** (The remainder of the battalion hereafter follows a separate lineage).

Assigned to the **80th Infantry Division.**

World War II Campaign Participation included **Northern France, Rhineland, Ardennes-Alsace** and **Central Europe.**

1945	**Meritorious Unit Commendation (Army),** with Streamer embroidered **EUROPEAN THEATER,** awarded to the **780th Ordnance Light Maintenance Company.**
1946	Inactivated at Camp Kilmer, New Jersey.

Redesignated as the **780th Airborne Ordnance Maintenance Company.**
Assigned to the **80th Airborne Division.**

1952   Reorganized and redesignated as the **780th Ordnance Maintenance Company.**
Assigned to the **80th Infantry Division.**

Reorganized and redesignated as **HHD, 780th Ordnance Battalion,** (with all organic elements concurrently constituted and activated).

1959   Disbanded at Richmond, Virginia.

1967   **HHD, 780th Ordnance Battalion** reconstituted in the Army Reserve, and redesignated as **HHD, 4th Brigade, 80th Division (Training).**

1968   Activated at Norfolk, Virginia.

1979   Relocated to Fort Story, Virginia.

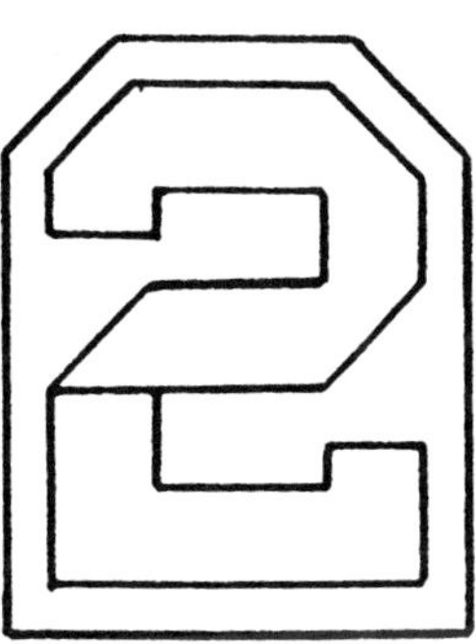

Second US Army SSI

HHC, 82d Airborne Division

HQ, 82d Abn Div
and NCBU DUI
1942

82d Abn Div SSI
Flash and Oval

82d Abn Div SSI

1917	Constituted in the National Army as **HQ, 82d Division.** Organized at Camp Gordon, Georgia. World War I Campaign Participation included **St Mihiel, Meuse-Argonne** and **Lorraine 1918.**
1919	Demobilized at Camp Mills, New York.
1921	Reconstituted in the Organized Reserves as **HQ, 82d Division.** Organized at Columbia, South Carolina.
1942	Redesignated as **Division Headquarters, 82d Division.** Ordered into Active Military Service. Reorganized at Camp Claiborne, Louisiana. Reorganized and redesignated as **HQ, 82d Airborne Division.** World War II Campaign Participation included **Sicily, Normandy** (with arrowhead), **Rhineland** (with arrowhead), **Ardennes-Alsace** and **Central Europe.**
1944	**Presidential Unit Citation (Army)**, with Streamer embroidered **STE MERE EGLISE**, awarded to **HQ, 82d Airborne Division.**
1948	Withdrawn from the Organized Reserve Corps and allotted to the Regular Army.
1950	French **Croix de Guerre with Palm, WW II**, with Streamer embroidered **STE MERE EGLISE**, awarded to **HQ, 82d Airborne Division.**

French **Croix de Guerre with Palm, WW II**, with Streamer embroidered **COTENTIN**, awarded to **HQ, 82d Airborne Division.**

French **Croix de Guerre, WW II, Fourragere,** awarded to **HQ, 82d Airborne Division.**

Belgian **Fourregere 1940,** awarded to **HQ, 82d Airborne Division.**

      82d Airborne Division Cited in the **Orders of the Day** of the Belgian Army for actions in the **ARDENNES.**
      82d Airborne Division Cited in the **Orders of the Day** of the Belgian Army for actions in **BELGIUM AND GERMANY.**

Military Order of William (Degree of the Knight of the Fourth Class), with Streamer embroidered **NIJMEGEN 1944,** awarded to **HQ, 82d Airborne Division.**

Netherlands **Orange Lanyard** awarded to **HQ, 82d Airborne Division.**

1964	Reorganized and redesignated as **HHC, 82d Airborne Division.**
1965	Deployed on Operation **POWER PACK** to the Dominican Republic. Last elements redeployed to Fort Bragg, North Carolina.
1983	Deployed to Grenada.
1984	All elements of the **82d Airborne Division** finally redeployed to Fort Bragg, North Carolina.

Armed Forces Expeditionary Streamer, embroidered **GRENADA**, awarded to HHC, **82d Airborne Division.**

NOTE: The **82d Airborne Division DUI** was approved for **HHC, 82d Airborne Division** on 23 October 1942; further approved for the **Command and Control Battalion, 82d Airborne Division** on 21 April 1958; and authorized for non-color-bearing units (NCBU) on 6 June 1966.

HHC, 1st Brigade, 82d Airborne Division

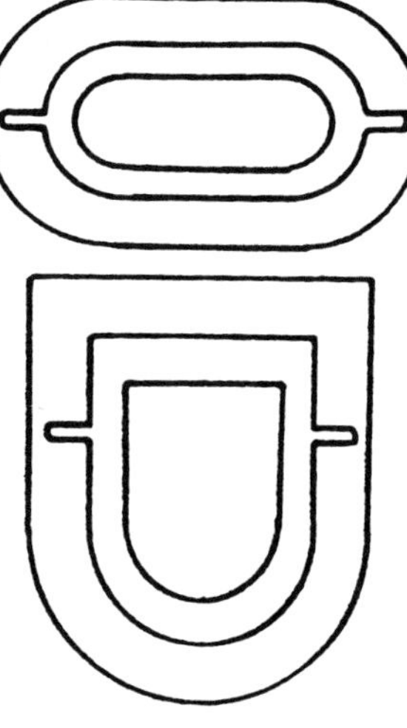

**HQ, 82d Abn Div
and NCBU DUI
1942**

**1st Bde, 82d Abn Div
Oval and Flash**

82d Abn Div SSI

1917	Constituted in the National Army as **HQ Troop, 82d Division**. Organized at Camp Gordon, Georgia. World War II Campaign Participation included **St Mihiel, Meuse-Argonne** and **Lorraine 1918.**
1919	Demobilized at Camp Mills, New York.
1921	Reconstituted in the Organized Reserves as **HQ Company, 82d Division.**
1922	Organized at Columbia, South Carolina.
1942	Reorganized and redesignated as **HQ and Military Police Company** (less the Military Police Platoon), **82d Division.** Ordered into Active Military Service. Reorganized at Camp Claiborne, Louisiana. Reorganized and redesignated as **HQ Company, 82d Airborne Division.** World War II Campaign Participation included **Sicily, Naples-Foggia, Normandy** (with arrowhead), **Rhineland** (with arrowhead), **Ardennes-Alsace** and **Central Europe.**
1944	**Presidential Unit Citation (Army),** with Streamer embroidered **STE MERE EGLISE,** awarded to **HQ Company, 82d Airborne Division.**
1948	Withdrawn from the Organized Reserves and allotted to the Regular Army.
1950	French **Croix de Guerre with Palm, WW II,** with Streamer embroidered **STE MERE**

EGLISE , awarded to **HQ Company, 82d Airborne Division.**

French **Croix de Guerre with Palm, WW II,** with Streamer embroidered **COTENTIN**, awarded to **HQ Company, 82d Airborne Division.**

French **Croix de Guerre, WW II, with Fourragere**, awarded to **HQ Company, 82d Airborne Division.**

Belgian **Fourragere 1940,** awarded to **HQ Co, 82d Airborne Division**

       82d Airborne Division Cited in the **Orders of the Day** of the Belgian Army, for actions in the **ARDENNES.**

       82d Airborne Division Cited in the **Orders of the Day** of the Belgian Army for actions in **BELGIUM AND GERMANY.**

Military Order of William (Degree of Knight of the Fourth Order), with Streamer embroidered **NIJMEGEN 1944,** awarded to **HQ Company, 82d Airborne Division.**

Netherlands **Orange Lanyard** awarded to **HQ Company, 82d Airborne Division.**

1957	Reorganized and redesignated as **HHC, Command and Control Battalion, 82d Airborne Division.**
1964	Reorganized and redesignated as **HHC, 1st Brigade, 82d Airborne Division.**
1965	Participated in Operation **POWER PACK.** Deployed with **HQ, 82d Airborne Division** to the Domican Republic.
1966	Last elements redeployed to Fort Bragg, North Carolina.
1967	Deployed to Washington, DC to assisting the quelling of civil disturbances. Redeployed to Fort Bragg, North Carolina.
1983	Deployed to Grenada.
1984	Last elements returned to Fort Bragg, NC.

       Armed Forces Expeditionary Streamer, embroidered **GRENADA,** awarded to the **1s Brigade, 82d Airborne Division.**

HHC, 2d Brigade, 82d Airborne Division

**HQ, 82d Abn Div
and NCBU DUI
1942**

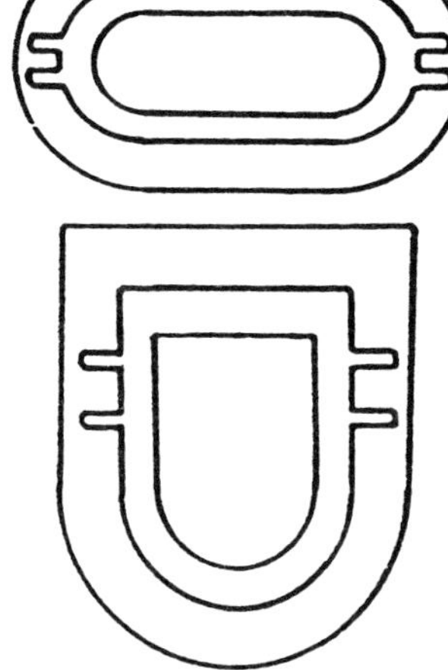

**2d Bde, 82d Abn Div
Oval and Flash**

82d Abn Div SSI

1917	Constituted in the National Army as **HQ, 155th Infantry Brigade.** Assigned to the **78th Division.** Organized at Camp Dix, New Jersey. World War II Campaigns included **St Mihiel, Meusse-Argonne** and **Lorraine 1918.**
1919	Demobilized at Camp Dix, New Jersey.
1921	Reconstituted in the Organized Reserves as **HHC, 155th Infantry Brigade.** Assigned to the **78th Division.** Organized at Elizabeth, New Jersey.
1925	Redesignated as **HHC, 155th Brigade.**
1936	Redesignated as **HHC, 155th Infantry Brigade.**
1942	Converted and redesignated as the **78th Reconnaissance Troop** (less 3d Platoon), **78th Division.** (**HHC, 156th Infantry Brigade** was concurrently converted and redesignated as the **3d Platoon, 78th Reconnaissance Troop**). Assigned to the **78th Division.** Ordered into Active Military Service. Reorganized at Camp Butner, North Carolina. Redesignated as the **78th Cavalry Reconnaissance Troop, 78th Division.**
1943	Reorganized and redesignated as the **78th Reconnaissance Troop, Mechanized.**

World War II Campaign Participation included the **Rhineland, Ardennes-Alsace** and **Central Europe.**

1945	Reorganized and redesignated as the **78th Mechanized Cavalry Reconnaissance Troop.**

1945   Reorganized and redesignated as the **78th Mechanized Cavalry Reconnaissance Troop.**

1946   Inactivated in Germany.

1947   Allocated to the Organized Reserves.
Assigned to the **78th Infantry Division.**
Activated at Plainfield, New Jersey.
Relocated to Newark, New Jersey.

1949   Reorganized and redesignated as the **78th Reconnaissance Company.**

1951   Relocated to Irvington, New Jersey.

1959   Disbanded at Irvington, New Jersey.

1963   Reconstituted (less **3d Platoon, 78th Reconnaissance Company**), as HHC, 155th Infantry **Brigade.**(3d Platoon hereafter folows a separate lineage).

1964   Redesignated as **HHC, 2d Brigade, 82d Airborne Division.**
Activated at Fort Bragg, North Carolina.

1965   Participated in Operation **POWER PACK.**
Deployed with the **82d Airborne Division** to the Dominican Republic.
Redeployed to Fort Bragg, North Carolina.

1983   Deployed with the **82d Airborne Division** to Grenada.

1984   Last elements redeployed to Fort Bragg, North Carolina.

Armed Forces Expeditionary Streamer, embroidered **GRENADA,** awarded to HHC, 2d Brigade, **82d Airborne Division.**

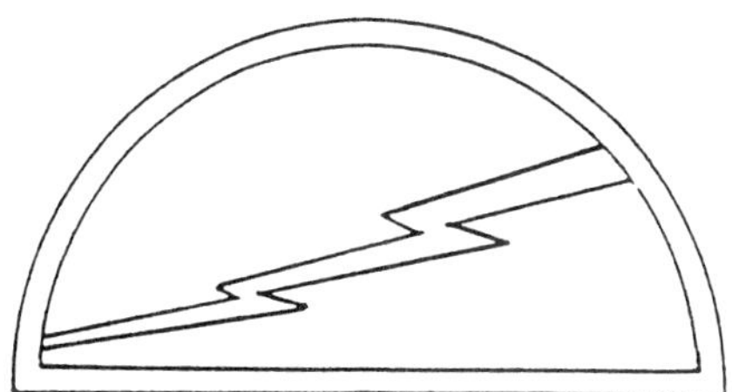

78th Infantry Div SSI
(redesignated as the 78th Divivision (Tng) on 1 May 1959)

HHC, 3d Brigade, 82d Airborne Division

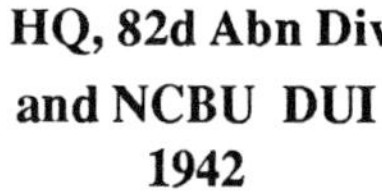

**HQ, 82d Abn Div
and NCBU DUI
1942**

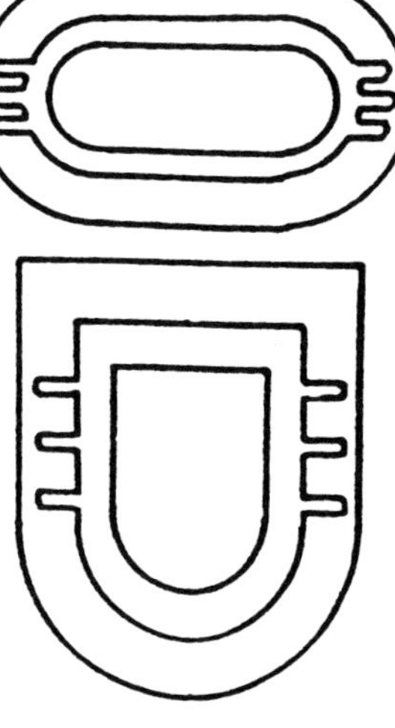

**3d Bde, 82d Abn Div
Oval and Flash**

82d Abn Div SSI

1917	Constituted in the National Army as **HQ, 156th Infantry Brigade.**
	Assigned to the **78th Division.** Organized at Camp Dix, New Jersey.
	World War I Campaign Participation included **St Mihiel, Meusse-Argonne** and **Lorraine 1918**
1919	Demobilized at Camp Dix, New Jersey.
1921	Reconstituted in the Orgainized Resrves as **HHC, 156th Infantry Brigade.** Assigned to the **78th Division.** Organized at Newark, New Jersey.
1925	Redesignated as **HHC, 156th Brigade.**
1936	Redesignated as **HHC, 156th Infantry Brigade.**
1942	Converted and redesignated as the **3d Platoon, 78th Reconnaissance Troop.** Assigned to the **78th Division.** (**HHC, 155th Infantry Brigade** concurrently converted and redesignated as the **78th Reconnaissance Troop**, minus the 3d Platoon).
	Ordered into Active Military Service.
	Reorganized at Camp Butner, North Carolina. Redesignated as the **78th Cavalry Reconnaissance Troop.** Assigned to the **78th Infantry Division.**

1943	Reorganized and redesignated as the **78th Reconnaissance Troop, Mechanized.**
	World War II Campaigns included the **Rhineland, Ardennes-Alsace** and **Central Europe.**
1945	Reorganized and redesignated as the **78th Mechanized Cavalry Reconnaissance Troop.**
1946	Inactivated in Germany.
1947	Allocated to the Organized Reserves. Assigned to the **78th Infantry Division** Activated at Plainfield, New Jersey. Relocated to Newark, New Jersey.
1949	Reorganized and redesignated as the **78th Reconnaissance Company.** Relocated to Irvington, New Jersey
1953	Inactivated at Irvington, New Jersey.
1959	Disbanded.
1963	**3d Platoon, 78th Reconnaissance Company,** reconstituted in the Regular Army. Redesignated as **HHC, 156th Infantry Brigade.** (Remainder of the **78th Reconnaissance Company** hereafter follows a separate lineage).
1964	Redesignated as **HHC, 3d Brigade, 82d Airborne Division.** Activated at Fort Bragg, North Carolina.
1965	Participated in Operation **POWER PACK.** Deployed with the **82d Airborne Division** to the Dominican Republic. Redeployed to Fort Bragg, North Carolina.
1967	Deployed to Detroit, Michigan to assist in quelling civil disturbances. Redeployed to Fort Bragg, North Carolina.
1968	Deployed to the Republic of Vietnam. Vietnam Campaign Particpation included the **Tet Offensive; Counteroffensive Phases IV, V** and **VI; Tet 69/Counteroffensive;** and **Summer-Fall 1969.**
1969	Redeployed to Fort Bragg, North Carolina.
1970	Republic of Vietnam **Cross of Gallantry, with Palm,** with Streamer embroidered **VIETNAM 1968-1969**, awarded to **HHC, 3d Brigade, 82d Airborne Division.**
1971	Republic of Vietnam **Civic Action Honor Medal** with Streamer embroidered **VIETNAM 1968** awarded to **HHC, 3d Brigade, 82d Airborne Division.**
1983	Deployed with the **82d Airborne Division** to Grenada.
1984	Last elements redeployed to Fort Bragg, North Carolina. **Armed Forces Expeditionary Streamer,** embroidered **GRENADA,** awarded to **HHC, 3d Brigade, 82d Airborne Division.**

HHC, 4th Brigade, 82d Airborne Division

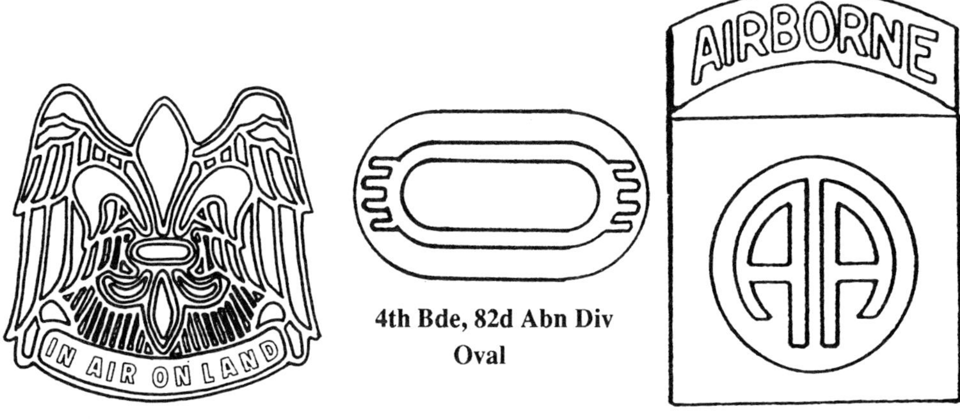

**82d Abn Div
and NCBU DU I
1942**

**4th Bde, 82d Abn Div
Oval**

82d Abn Div SSI

1968   Constituted in the Regular Army as **HHC, 4th Brigade, 82d Airborne Division.** Activated at Fort Bragg, North Carolina.

1969   Inactivated at Fort Bragg, North Carolina.

NOTE: The **4th Brigade, 82d Airborne Division** was activated during the period that the **3d Brigade** was deployed to the Republic of Vietnam. This was to enable the **82d Airborne Division** to field a full Division if required to respond to National Command Authority deployment directives. During this period, the maroon beret was not worn by the **82d Airborne Division**, thus no beret flash was manufactured.

HQ, 84th Airborne Division

84th Inf Div DUI
1942   **84th Abn Div SSI**

1917	Constituted in the National Army as **HQ, 84th Division** Organized at Camp Zachary Taylor, Kentucky. World War I Campaign Participation provided a Streamer without inscription.
1919	Demobilized at Camp Zachary Taylor, Kentucky.
1921	Reconstituted in the Organized Reserves. Redesignated as **HQ, 84th Division.** Organized at Indianapolis, Indiana.
1942	Redesignated as **Division HQ, 84th Division.** Ordered into Active Military Service. Reorganized at Camp Howze, Texas. Redesignated as **HQ, 84th Infantry Division.** World War II Campaigns included **Rhineland, Ardennes-Alsace** and **Central Europe.**
1946	Inactivated at Camp Kilmer, New Jersey. Redesignated as **HQ, 84th Airborne Division.** Assigned to **Fifth Army.**
1947	Activated at Madison, Wisconsin. Relocated to Milwaukee, Wisconsin.
1948	Relocated to Madison, Wisconsin.
1952	Reorganized and redesignated as **HQ, 84th Infantry Division.**
1957	Relocated to Milwaukee, Wisconsin.
1959	Reorganized and redesignated as **HHC, 84th Division (Training).**
1984	Relieved from assignment to **Fifth US Army.** Assigned to **Fourth US Army.**

HHD, 1st Bde,
84th Division (Training)
(HQ Company, 84th Airborne Division)

84th Inf Div DUI
1942

84th Airborne Div SSI

1917	Constituted in the National Army as **HQ Troop, 84th Division.** Organized at Camp Zachary Taylor, Kentucky. World War I Campaign Participation provided a Streamer without inscription.
1918	Demobilized in France.
1921	Reconstituted in the Organized Reserves, and redesignated as **HQ Company, 84th Division**
1922	Organized at Indianapolis, Indiana.
1942	Reorganized and redesignated as **HQ and Military Police Company** (less the M P Platoon). Ordered into Active Military Service, reorganized at Camp Howze, Tx as **HQ Co, 84th Inf Div.** World War II Campaigns included the **Rhineland, Ardennes-Alsace** and **Central Europe.**
1945	**Meritorious Unit Commendation (Army),** with Streamer embroidered **EUROPEAN THEATER,** awarded to **HQ Company, 84th Infantry Division.**
1946	Inactivated, reorganized and redsignated at Camp Kilmer, New Jersey as **HQ Co, 84th Abn Div.**
1947	Activated at Madison, Wisconsin.
1952	Reorganized and redesignated as **HQ Company, 84th Infantry Division.**
1957	Relocated to Milwaukee, Wisconsin.
1959	Disbanded at Milwaukee, Wisconsin.
1967	Reconstituted in the Army Reserves as **HHD, 1st Brigade, 84th Division (Training).**
1968	Activated at Milwaukee, Wisconsin.
1978	Reorganized and redesignated as **HHC, 1st Brigade, 84th Division (Training).**
1982	Reorganized and redesignated as **HQ, 1st Brigade, 84th Division (Training).**
1984	Reorganized and redesignated as **HHD, 1st Brigade, 84th Division (Training).**

HHD, 2d Brigade,
84th Division (Training)
(909th Airborne Field Artillery Battalion)

84th Div (Tng) DUI

909th Abn FA Bn DUI

84th Abn Div SSI

1917	Constituted in the National Army as the **309th Ammunition Train.** Assigned to the **84th Division.** Organized at Camp Zachary Taylor, Kentucky. World War I Campaign Participation provided a Streamer without inscription.
1919	Demobilized at Camp Sherman, Ohio.
1936	Reconstituted in the Organized Reserves. Concurrently consolidated with the **309th Ammunition Train** (activated inthe Organized Reserves in 1921 at Fort Wayne, Indiana), with the consolidated unit designated as the **309th Ammunition Train, 84th Division.**
1942	Converted and redesignated as the **909th Field Artillery Battalion.** Assigned to the **84th Division** Ordered into Active Military Service, reorganized at Camp Howze, Texas. World War II Campiagns included the **Rhineland, Ardennes-Alsace** and **Central Europe.**
1946	Inactivated at Camp Kilmer, New Jersey. Redesignated as the **909th Parachute Field Artillery Battalion, 84th Airborne Division.**
1947	Allotted to the Organized Reserves, activated at Sheboygan, Wisconsin.
1951	Reorganized and redesignated as the **909th Airborne Field Artillery Battalion.**
1952	Reorganized and redesignated as the **909th Field Artillery Battalion, 84th Infantry Division.**
1959	Disbanded at Sheboygan, Wisconsin.
1967	**HHB, 909th Field Artillery Battalion** reconstituted in the Army Reserve. Reorganized and redesignated as **HHD, 2d Brigade, 84th Division (Training).**
1968	Activated at Beaver Dam, Wisconsin.
1978	Reorganized and redesignated as **HHC, 2d Brigade, 84th Division (Training).**
1982	Reorganized and redesignated as **HQ, 2d Brigade, 84th Division (Training).**
1984	Reorganized and redesignated as **HHD, 2d Brigade, 84th Division (Training).**

HHD, 3d Brigade, 84th Division (Training)
(309th Airborne Engineer Battalion)

84th Inf Div DUI
1942

309th Abn Engr Bn DUI

84th Abn Div SSI

1917	Organized in the National Army as the **309th Engineers.**
	Assigned to the **84th Division.**
	Organized at Camp Zachary Taylor, Kentucky.
	World War I Campaign Participation provided a Streamer without inscription.
1919	Demobilized at Camp Sherman, Ohio.
1936	Reconstituted in the Organized Reserves.
	Concurrently consolidated with the **309th Engineers,** (activated in 1921 in Indianapolis, Indiana; relocated in 1931 to Terre Haute, Indiana; returning in 1934 to Indianapolis, Indiana). The consolidated unit designated as the **309th Engineers.** Assigned to the **84th Division.**
1942	Redesignated (less the 2d Battalion), as the **309th Engineer Battalion.**
	(The **2d Battalion, 309th Engineers** hereafter follows a separate lineage).
	Ordered into Active Military Service, reorganized at Camp Howze, Texas.
1943	Reorganized and redesignated as the **309th Engineer Combat Battalion.**
	World War II Campaigns included the **Rhineland, Ardennes-Alsace** and **Central Europe.**
1945	**Meritorious Unit Commendation (Army),** with Streamer embroidered **EUROPEAN THEATER,** awarded to HSC, **309th Engineer Combat Battalion.**
1946	Inactivated at Camp Kilmer, New Jersey, allotted to the Organized Reserves.
	Redesignated as the **309th Airborne Engineer Bn,** assigned to the **84th Airborne Division.**
1947	Activated at Milwaukee, Wisconsin.
1952	Reorganized and redesignated as the **309th Engineer Combat Battalion, 84th Inf Division.**
1953	Reorganized and redesignated as as the **309th Engineer Battalion.**
1959	Disbanded, (less Companies A and B), at Milwaukee, Wisconsin.
	(**Companies A and B, 309th Engineer Battalion,** hereafter follow a separate lineage.
1967	**HHSC, 309th Engr Bn** reconstituted in the Army Reserve, as **HHD, 3d Bde, 84th Div (Tng).**
1968	Activated at Milwaukee, Wisconsin.
1971	Reorganized and redesignated as **HHC, 3d Brigade, 84th Division (Training).**
1982	Reorganized and redesignated as **HQ, 3d Brigade, 84th Division (Training).**
1984	Reorganized and redesignated as **HHD, 3d Brigade, 84th Division (Training)**

HHD, 4th Brigade,
84th Division (Training)
(784th Airborne Ordnance Maintenance Co)

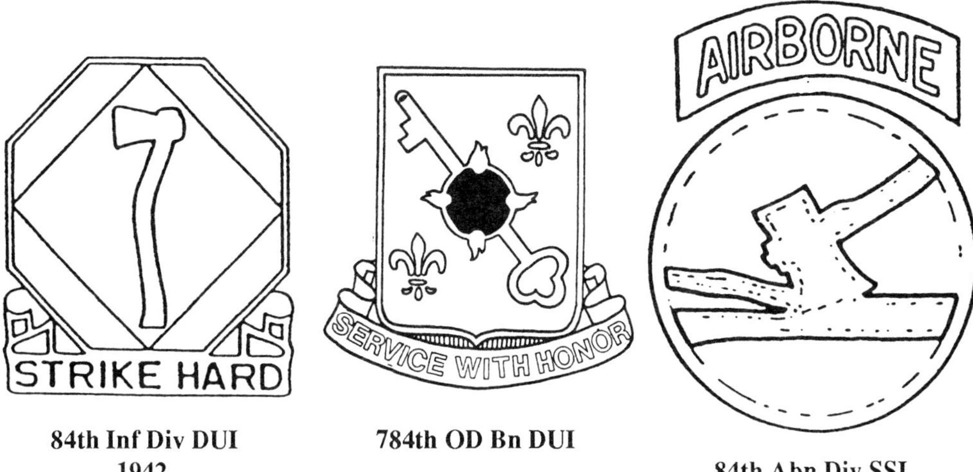

84th Inf Div DUI
1942

784th OD Bn DUI

84th Abn Div SSI

1917	Constituted in the National Army as the **309th Supply Train.** Assigned to the **84th Division.** Organized at Camp Zachary Taylor, Kentucky. World War I Campaign Participation provided a Streamer without inscription.
1919	Demobilized at Camp Sherman, Ohio.
1936	Reconstituted in the Organized Reserves. Concurrently consolidated with the **409th Quartermaster Regiment** (activated in 1921 in the Organized Reserves as the **84th Division Train, Quartermaster Corps**, at Indianapolis, Indiana; again redesignated in 1925 as the **84th Division Quartermaster Train**; and further designated as the **409th Quartermaster Regiment** in 1936). The consolidated unit designated as the **409th Quartermaster Regiment.** Assigned to the **84th Division.**
1942	Redesignated as the **409th Quartermaster Battalion.** The **Ordnance Maintenance Platoon, HQ Company, 409th Quartermaster Battalion,** redesignated as the **784th Ordnance Light Mainteance Company.** (Remainder of the **409th Quartermaster Battalion** hereafter follows a separate lineage). Ordered into Active Military Service. Reorganized at Camp Howze, Texas. World War II Campaign Participation included the **Rhineland, Ardennes-Alsace** and **Central Europe.**

| 1945 | **Meritorious Unit Commendation (Army)**, with Streamer embroidered **EUROPEAN THEATER**, awarded to the **784th Ordnance Light Maintenance Company.** |

1945   **Meritorious Unit Commendation (Army)**, with Streamer embroidered **EUROPEAN THEATER**, awarded to the **784th Ordnance Light Maintenance Company.**

1946   Inactivated at Camp Kilmer, New Jersey.
Allotted to the Organized Reserves.
Reorganized and redesignated as the **784th Airborne Ordnance Maintenance Company.**
Assigned to the **84th Airborne Division.**

1947   Activated at Milwaukee, Wisconsin.

1952   Reorganized and redesignated as the **784th Ordnance Maintenance Company.**
Assigned to the **84th Infantry Division.**

1953   Reorganized and redesignated as **HHD, 784th Ordnance Battalion,** (with organic elements concurrently constituted and activated.

1959   Disbanded at Milwaukee, Wisconsin.

1967   **HHD, 784th Ordnance Battalion** reconstituted in the Army Reserve.
Reorganized and redesignated as **HHD, 4th Brigade, 84th Division (Training).**

1968   Activated at Milwaukee, Wisconsin.

1978   Reorganized and redesignated as **HHC, 4th Brigade, 84th Division (Training).**

1982   Reorganized and redesignated as **HQ, 4th Brigade, 84th Division (Training).**

1984   Reorganized and redesignated as **HHD, 4th Brigade, 84th Division (Training).**

NOTE: The **84th Infantry Division DUI** was approved and authorized on 23 December 1942, and redesignated for the **84th Division (Training),** on 16 January 1967.

HQ, 100th Airborne Division

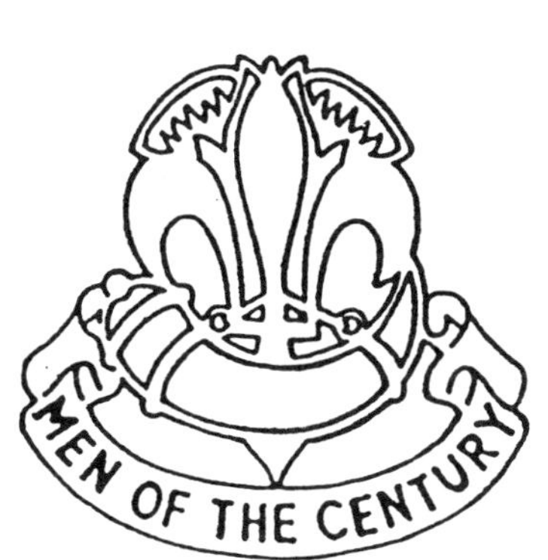

100th Div (Tng) DUI
1968

100th Abn Div SSI

1918	Constituted in the National Army as **HQ, 100th Division.** Organized and demobilized at Camp Bowie, Texas.
1921	Reconstituted in the Organized Reserves as **HQ, 100th Division.** Organized at Charleston, West Virginia.
1924	Relocated to Huntington, West Virginia.
1937	Relocated to Charleston, West Virginia.
1942	Redesignated as **Division HQ, 100th Division.** Ordered into Active Military Service. Reorganized at Fort Jackson, South Carolina. Redesignated as **HQ, 100th Infantry Division.** World War II Campaigns included the **Rhineland, Ardennes-Alsace** and **Central Europe.**
1946	Inactivated at Camp Patrick Henry, Virginia. Allotted to the Organized Reserves. Reorganized and redesignated as **HQ, 100th Airborne Division.** Assigned to **Second Army.** Activated at Louisville, Kentucky.
1952	Reorganized and redesignated as **HQ, 100th Infantry Division.**
1959	Reorganized and redesignated as **HHC, 100th Division (Training).**
1961	Ordered into Active Military Service.
1962	Released from Active Military Service.
1966	Reassigned from **Second US Army** to **First US Army.**
1973	Reassigned from **First US Army** to **Fifth US Army.**
1983	Reassigned from **Fifth US Army** to **Second US Army.**

HHD, 1st Brigade, 100th Division (Training)
(HQ Company, 100th Airborne Division)

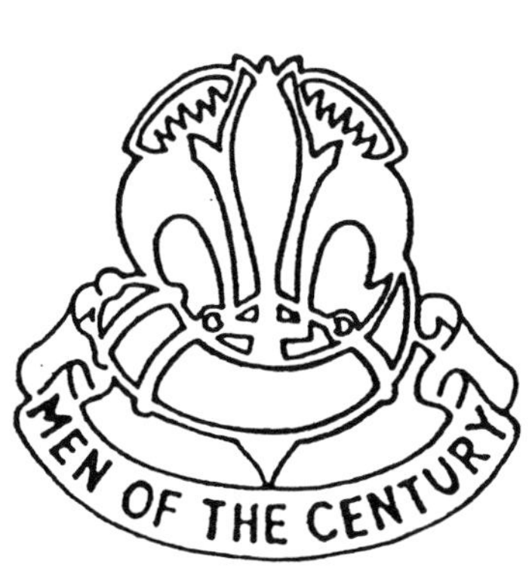

**100th Div (Tng) DUI
1968**

100th Airborne Div SSI

1921	Constituted in the Organized Reserves as **HQ Company, 100th Division.**
1922	Organized at Charleston, West Virginia.
1924	Relocated to Huntington, West Virginia.
1942	Reorganized and redesignated as **HQ and Military Police Co,** (less the M P Platoon), **100th Div** Ordered into Active Military Service. Reorganized at Fort Jackson, South Carolina. World War II Campaigns included the **Rhineland, Ardennes-Alsace** and **Central Europe.**
1946	Inactivated at Camp Patrick Henry, Virginia. Allotted to the Organized Reserves. Redesignated as **HQ Company, 100th Airborne Division.** Activated at Louisville, Kentucky.
1952	Reorganized and redesignated as **HQ Company, 100th Infantry Division.**
1959	Disbanded at Louisville, Kentucky.
1967	Reconstituted in the Army Reserve as **HHD, 1st Bde, 100th Div (Tng).**
1968	Activated at Lexington, Kentucky.

NOTE: The **100th Division (Training) DUI** was authorized for the **HQ, 100th Division (Training),** the **Command and Control Battalion,** and non color bearing units (NCBU), in 1968.

HHD, 2d Brigade, 100th Division (Training)
(925th Airborne Field Artillery Battalion)

**100th Div (Tng) DUI
1968**

**925th Abn FA Bn DUI
1950**

100th Abn Div SSI

1921	Constituted in the Organized Reserves as the **325th Ammunition Train**. Assigned to the **100th Division**. Organized at Charleston, West Virginia.
1922	Relocated to Sheperdstown, West Virginia.
1924	Relocated to Charleston, West Virginia,
1929	Relocated to Huntington, West Virginia.
1931	Relocated to Parkersburg, West Virginia.
1942	Converted and redesignated as the **925th Field Artillery Battalion, 100th Division**. Ordered into Active Military Service. Reorganized at Fort Jackson, South carolina. World War II Campaigns included the **Rhineland, Ardennes- Alsace** amd **Cenral Europe**.
1946	Inactivated at Camp Patrick Henry, Virginia. Redesignated as the **925th Glider Field Artillery Battalion**. Assigned to the **100th Airborne Division**. Activated at Lexington, Kentucky.
1950	Reorganized and redesignated as the **925th Airborne Field Artillery Battalion**.
1952	Reorganized and redesignated as the **925th Field Artillery Battalion**. Assigned to the **100th Infantry Division**.
1959	Disbanded at Lexington, Kentucky.
1967	**HHB, 925th Artillery Battalion** reconstituted in the Army Reserve. Redesignated as **HHD, 2d Brigade, 100th Division (Training)**.
1968	Activated at Owensboro, Kentucky.

HHD, 3d Brigade,
100th Division (Training)
(325th Airborne Engineer Battalion)

100th Div (Tng) DUI 1968

325th Engr Bn DUI

100th Airborne Div SSI

1921	Constituted in the Organized Reserves as the **325th Engineers.** Assigned to the **100th Division.**, organized at Huntington, West Virginia.
1931	Relocated to Charleston , West Virginia.
1942	Redesignated (less 2d Battalion), as the **325th Engineer Battalion.** (The 2d Battalion hereafter follows a separate lineage). Ordered into Active Military Service, reorganized at Fort Jackson, South Carolina. Redesignated as the **325th Engineer Combat Battalion.** World War II Campaigns included the **Rhineland, Ardennes-Alsace** and **Central Europe.**
1945	**Meritorious Unit Commendation (Army)**, with Streamer embroidered **EUROPEAN THEATER,** awarded to **HSC, 325th Engineer Combat Battalion.**
1946	Inactivated at Camp Kilmer, New Jersey, resuming Organized Reserve status. Redesignated as the **325th Airborne Engineer Battalion.** Assigned to the **100th Airborne Division**, activated at Williamson, West Virginia.
1947	Relocated to Huntington, West Virginia.
1949	Relocated to Charleston, West Virginia.
1950	Relocated to Wheeling, West Virginia.
1952	Reorganized and redesignated as the **325th Engineer Combat Bn, 100th Infantry Division.**
1953	Reorganized and redesignated as the **325th Engineer Battalion.**
1954	Relocated to Fairmont, West Virginia.
1959	Disbanded, (less **Companies A** and **B**), at Fairmont, West Virginia. (**Companies A** and **B, 325th Engineer Battalion** hereafter follow a separate lineage).
1967	**HHSC, 325th Engr Bn**, reconstituted in the Army Reserve, as **HHD, 3d Bde, 100th Div (Tng).**
1968	Activated at Lexington, Kentucky.
1971	Reorganized and redesignated as HHC, **3d Brigade, 100th Division (Training)**
1973	Reorganized and redesignated as HHSC, **3d Brigade, 100th Division (Training).**
1978	Reorganized and redesignated as **HHD, 3d Brigade, 100th Division (Training).**

HHD, 4th Brigade,
100th Division (Training)
(800th Airborne Ordnance Maintenance Co)

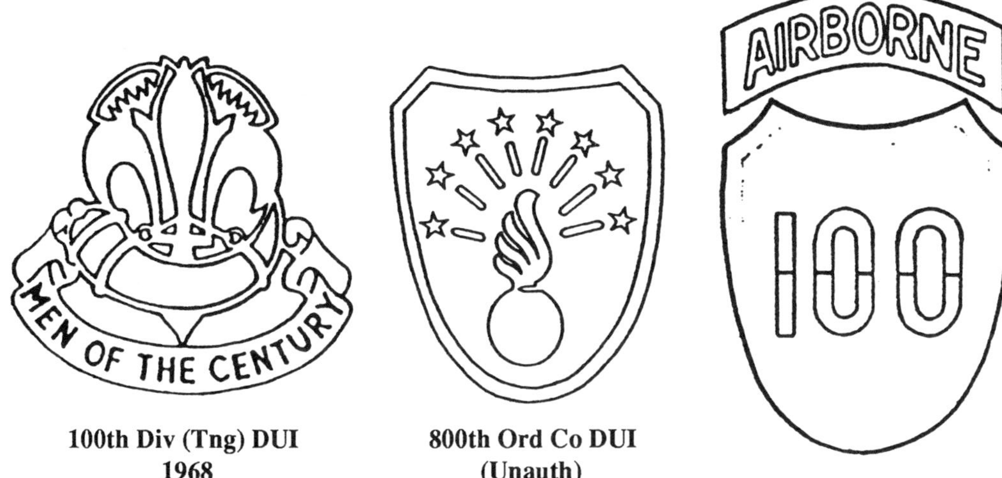

100th Div (Tng) DUI
1968

800th Ord Co DUI
(Unauth)

100th Abn Div SSI

1921	Constituted in the Organized Reserves as the **100th Division Train, Quartermaster Corps.** Organized at Huntington, West Virginia.
1925	Redesignated as the **100th Division Quartermaster Train.**
1929	Relocated to Wheeling, West Virginia.
1931	Relocated to Huntington, West Virginia.
1936	Redesignated as the **425th Quartermaster Regiment.** Assigned to the **100th Division.**
1942	Redesignated as the **425th Quartermaster Battalion.** The **Ordnance Maintenance Platoon, HQ Company, 425th Quartermaster Battalion,** redesignated as the **800th Ordnance Light Maintenance Company.** (The remainder of the **425th Quartermaster Battalion** hereafter follows a separate lineage). Assigned to the **100th Infantry Division.** Ordered into Active Military Service, reorganized at Fort Jackson, South Carolina. World War II Campaigns included the **Rhineland, Ardennes-Alsace** and **Central Europe.**
1945	**Meritorious Unit Commendation (Army),** with Streamer embroidered **EUROPEAN THEATER,** awarded to the **800th Ordnance Light Maintenance Company.**
1946	Inactivated at Camp Patrick Henry, Virginia, resuming Organized Reserve status Reorganized and redesignated as the **800th Airborne Ord Maint Co, 100th Airborne Div.** Activated at Buckhannon, West Virginia.
1949	Relocated to Morganstown, West Virginia.
1952	Reorganized and redesignated as the **800th Ordnance Maintenance Company, 100th Inf Div.** Reorganized and redesignated as **HHD, 800th Ordnance Battalion** (with organic elements concurrently constituted and activated).
1956	Relocated to Louisville, Kentucky.
1959	Disbanded at Louisville, Kentucky.
1967	**HHD, 800th Ord Bn** reconstituted in the Army Reserve, as **HHD, 4th Bde, 100th Div (Tng).**
1968	Activated at Louisville, Kentucky.
1973	Inactivated at Louisville, Kentucky.

HHC, 101st Airborne Division

HQ, 101st Abn Div
and NCBU DUI
1958

HQ, 101st Abn Div Oval

HQ, 101st Abn Div (Air
Assault) Flash 1972-76

101st Abn Div SSI

1918	Constituted in the National Army as **HQ, 101st Division**. Organized at Camp Shelby, Mississippi. Demobilized at Camp Shelby, Mississippi.
1921	Reconstituted in the Organized Reserves as **HQ, 101st Division**. Organized at Milwaukee, Wisconsin.
1942	Redesignated as **Division HQ, 101st Division**. Disbanded and concurrently reconstituted in the AUS. Redesignated as **HQ, 101st Airborne Division**. Activated at Camp Claiborne, Louisiana. World War II Campaign Participation included **Normandy** (with arrowhead), the **Rhineland** (with arrowhead), **Ardennes-Alsace** and **Central Europe**.
1945	Inactivated in France **Presidential Unit Citation**, with Streamer embroidered NORMANDY, awarded to **HQ, 101st Airborne Division**. **Presidential Unit Citation**, with Streamer embroidered BASTOGNE, awarded to **HQ, 101st Airborne Division**.
1948	Allotted to the Regular Army. Activated at Camp Breckinridge, Kentucky.
1949	Inactivated at Camp Breckinridge, Kentucky.

1950	Activated at Camp Breckinridge, Kentucky.

1950 — Activated at Camp Breckinridge, Kentucky.

French **Croix de Guerre with Palm, WW II,** with Streamer embroidered **NORMANDY,** awarded to **HQ, 101st Airborne Division.**

Belgian **Fourragere 1940**, awarded to **HQ 101st Airborne Division.**
    101st Airborne Division Cited in the **Orders of the Day** of the Belgian Army for actions in **FRANCE and BELGIUM**

Netherlands **Orange Lanyard** awarded to **HQ, 101st Airborne Division.**

1953 — Inactivated at Camp Breckinridge, Kentucky.

1954 — Activated at Fort Jackson, South Carolina.

1959 — Belgian **Croix de Guerre 1940, with Palm**, with Streamer embroidered **BASTOGNE,** awarded to **HQ, 101st Airborne Division.**
    101st Airborne Division Cited in the **Order of the Day** of the Belgian Army, for actions at **BASTOGNE.**

1964 — Reorganized and redesignated as **HHC, 101st Airborne Division.**

1967 — Deployed to the Republic of Vietnam.

Vietnam Campaign Participation included the **Tet Counteroffensive; Counteroffensive Phases III, IV, V, VI and VII; Tet 69/Counteroffensive; Summer-Fall 1969; Winter-Spring 1970; Sactuary Counteroffensive** and **Consolidations I and II.**

1969 — Reorganized and redesignated as **HHC, 101st Airborne Division (Airmobile).**

1970 — Republic of Vietnam **Cross of Gallantry with Palm**, with Streamer embroidered **VIETNAM 1968-1969,** awarded to **HHC, 101st Airborne Division.**

1971 — Republic of Vietnam **Civic Action Honor Medal, First Class**, with Streamer embroidered **VIETNAM 1968-1970,** awarded to **HHC, 101st Airborne Division.**

1972 — Redeployed to Fort Campbell, Kentucky.

1974 — Republic of Vietnam **Cross of Gallantry with Palm**, with Streamer **VIETNAM 1971**, awarded to the **101st Airborne Division.**

Redesignated as **HHC, 101st Airborne Division (Air Assault).**

HHC, 1st Brigade, 101st Airborne Division

HQ, 101st Abn Div
and NCBU DUI
1958

1st Bde 101st Abn Div
Airborne Oval

1st Bde 101st Abn Div (Air
Assault) Flash 1972-1976

101st Abn Div SSI

1921	Constituted in the Organized Reserves as **HQ Company, 101st Division**. Organized at Milwaukee, Wisconsin.
1942	Reorganized and redesignated as **HQ and Military Police Company** (less Military Police Platoon), **101st Division**. Disbanded and concurrently reconstituted in the AUS as **HQ Company, 101st Airborne Division**. Activated at Camp Claiborne, Louisiana.
	World War II Campaign Participation included **Normandy** (with arrowhead),the **Rhineland** (with arrowhead) , **Ardennes-Alsace** and **Central Europe**.
1945	Inactivated in France.
	Presidential Unit Citation (Army), with Streamer embroidered **NORMANDY**, awarded to **HQ Company, 101st Airborne Division**.
	Presidential Unit Citation (Army), with Streamer embroidered **BASTOGNE**, awarded to **HQ Company, 101st Airborne Division**.
1948	Allotted to the Regular Army. Activated at Camp Breckinridge, Kentucky.
1949	Inactivated at Camp Breckinridge, Kentucky.

1950   Activated at Camp Breckinridge, Kentucky.

               French **Croix de Guerre with Palm, WW II**, with Streamer embroideredNORMANDY,
               awarded to the **101st Airborne Division.**
               Belgian **Fourragere 1940**, awarded to **HQ Company, 101st Airborne Div.**
                       101st Airborne Division Cited in the **Order of The Day** of the Belgian Army for
               actions at **BASTOGNE.**

1964   Reorganized and redesignated as **HHC, 1st Brigade, 101st Airborne Div.**

1965   Deployed to the Republic of Vietnam.

               Vietnam Campaign Participation included the **Defense; Counteroffensive; Counteroffensive
               Phases II, II, IV, V, VI and VII; Tet Counteroffensive; Tet 69/Counteroffensive; Summer-
               Fall 1969; Winter-Spring 1970; Sanctuary Counteroffensive,** and Consolidations I and II

1968   **Presidential Unit Citation (Army),** with Streamer embroidered **DAK TO,** awarded to HHC,
               1st Brigade, 101st Airborne Division.

               Meritorious Unit Citation (Army), with Streamer embroidered **VIETNAM 1965-1966,**
               awarded to **HHC, 1st Brigade, 101st Airborne Division.**

1969   Reorganized and redesignated as **HHC, 1st Brigade, 101st Airborne Division (Airmobile).**

               Valorous Unit Award, with Streamer embroidered **TUY HOA,** awarded to HHC, 1st Brigade,
               101st Airborne Division.

               Republic of Vietnam **Cross of Gallantry with Palm,** with Streamer embroidered **VIETNAM
               1966-1967,** awarded to **HHC, 1st Brigade, 101st Airborne Division.**

1971   Republic of Vietnam **Cross of Gallantry with Palm,** with Streamer embroidered **VIETNAM
               1971,** awarded to **HHC, 1st Brigade, 101st Airborne Division.**

               Republic of Vietnam **Civic Action Honor Medal, First Class,** with Streamer embroidered
               VIETNAM 1968-1970, awarded to **HHC, 1stBrigade, 101st Airborne Division.**

1972   Redeployed to Fort Campbell, Kentucky.

1974   Redesignated as **HHC, 1st Brigade, 101st Airborne Division (Air Assault).**

pre 1958 101st Abn Div DUI
(also worn by HHC, 1st Brigade in RVN)

HHC, 2d Brigade,
101st Airborne Division

**2d Bde, 101st Abn Div
Airborne Oval**

**HQ, 101st Abn Div
and NCBU DUI
1958**

**2d Bde, 101st Abn Div (Air
Assault) Flash 1972-1976**

101st Airborne Div SSI

1917	Constituted in the National Army as **HQ, 159th Infantry Brigade.** Assigned to the **80th Division.** Organized at Camp Lee, Virginia.
	World War I Campaign Participation included the **Somme Offensive; Meuse-Argonne** and **Picardy 1918.**
1919	Demobilized at Camp Lee, Virginia.
1921	Reconstituted in the Organized Reserves as **HHC, 159th Infantry Brigade.** Assigned to the **80th Division.**
1922	Organized at Richmond, Virginia.
1925	Redesignated as **HHC, 159th Brigade.**
1936	Redesignated as **HHC, 159th Infantry Brigade.**
1942	Converted and redesignated as the **80th Reconnaissance Troop** (less the 3d Platoon), **80th Division.** (HHC, 160th Infantry Brigade** concurrently converted and redesignated as the **3d Platoon, 80th Reconnaissance Troop**).

1943	Ordered into Active Federal Service.

1943 Ordered into Active Federal Service.
      Reorganized at Camp Forrest, Tennessee.
      Redesignated as the **80th Cavalry Reconnaissance Troop, 80th Division.**
      Reorganized and redesignated as the **80th Reconnaissance Troop, Mechanized.**

      World War II Campaign Participation included **Northern France**, the**Rhineland, Ardennes-Alsace** and **Central Europe.**

1946 Inactivated at Camp Kilmer, New Jersey.
      Allotted to the Organized Reserves.
      Redesignated as the **Reconnaissance Platoon, 80th Airborne Division.**

1947 Redesignated as the **80th Airborne Reconnaissance Platoon.**
      Assigned to the **80th Airborne Division.**
      Activated at Richmond, Virginia.

1948 Reorganized and redesignated as the **Reconnaissance Platoon, 80th Airborne Division.**

1950 Reorganized and redesignated as the **80th Airborne Reconnaissance Company**

1952 Reorganized and redesignated as the **80th Reconnaissance Company.**

1959 Disbanded at Richmond, Virginia.

1963 Reconstituted (less 3d Platoon), in the Regular Army, as **HHC, 159th Infantry Brigade.**
      (The 3d Platoon hereafter follows a separate lineage).

1964 Redesignated as **HHC, 2d Brigade, 101st Airborne Division.**
      Activated at Fort Campbell, Kentucky.

1967 Deployed with the **101st Airborne Division** to the Republic of Vietnam.

1969 Reorganized and redesignated as the **2d Bde, 101st Airborne Div (Airmobile).**

      Vietnam Campaign Participation included the **Tet Counteroffensive; Counteroffensive Phases III, IV, V, VI and VII; Tet 69/Counteroffensive; Summer-Fall 1969; Winter-Spring 1970; Sanctuary Counteroffensive** and **Consolidations I and II.**
      Republic of Vietnam **Cross of Gallantry with Palm**, with Streamer embroidered **VIETNAM 1968,** awarded to **HHC, 2d Brigade, 101st Airborne Division.**

1970 Republic of Vietnam **Cross of Gallantry with Palm**, with Streamer embroidered **VIETNAM 1968,** awarded to **HHC, 2d Brigade, 101st Airborne Division.**

1971 Republic of Vietnam **Civic Action Honor Medal, First Class**, with Streamer embroidered **VIETNAM 1968-1970**, awarded to **HHC, 2d Brigade, 101st Airborne Division.**

1972 Redeployed to Fort Campbell, Kentucky.

1974 Republic of Vietnam, **Cross of Gallantry with Palm**, with Streamer embroidered **VIETNAM 1971**, awarded to **HHC, 2d Brigade, 101st Airborne Division.**
      Redesignated as **HHC, 2d Brigade, 101st Airborne Division (Air Assault).**

HHC, 3d Brigade, 101st Airborne Division

HQ, 101st Abn Div
and NCBU DUI
1958

3d Bde, 101st Abn Div
Airborne Oval

3d Bde, 101st Abn Div (Air
Assault) Flash 1972-76

101st Airborne Div SSI

1917	Constituted in the National Army as **HQ, 160th Infantry Brigade.** Assigned to the **80th Division.** Ognaized at Camp Lee, Virginia. World War I Campaign Participation included the **Somme Offensive, Meuse-Argonne** and **Picardy 1918.**
1919	Demobilized at Camp Lee, Virginia.
1921	Reconstituted in the Organized Reserves. Redesignated as **HHC, 160th Infantry Brigade.**
1922	Organized at Baltimore, Maryland.
1925	Redesignated as **HHC, 160th Brigade.**
1936	Redesignated as **HHC, 160th Infantry Brigade.**
1942	Converted and redesignated as the **3d Platoon, 80th Reconnaissance Troop, 80th Division.** (**HHC, 159th Infantry Brigade** concurrently converted and redesignated as the **80th Reconnaissance Troop** - less the 3d Platoon). Ordered into Active Military Service. Reorganized at Camp Forrest, Tennessee. Redesignated as the **80th Cavalry Reconnaissance Troop.**

1943   Reorganized and redesignated as the **80th Reconnaissance Troop, Mechanized.**

World War II Campaign Participation included **Northern France, Rhineland, Ardennes-Alsace** and **Central Europe.**

1946   Inactivated at Camp Kilmer, New Jersey.
Redesignated as the **Reconnaissance Platoon, 80th Airborne Division.**

1947   Activated at Richmond, Virginia.
Redesignated as the **80th Airborne Reconnaissance Platoon.**
Assigned to the **80th Airborne Division.**

1948   Reorganized and redesignated as the **Reconnaissance Platoon, 80th Airborne Division.**

1950   Reorganized and redesignated as as the **80th Airborne Reconnaissance Company.**

1952   Reorganized and redesignated as the **80th Reconnaissance Company.**
Assigned to the **80th Infantry Division.**

1959   Disbanded at Richmond, Virginia.

1963   **3d Platoon, 80th Reconnaissance Company**, reconstituted in the Regular Army as **HHC, 160th Infantry Brigade.**
(The remainder of the **80th Reconnaissance Company** hereafter follows a separate lineage).

1964   Redesignated as **HHC, 3d Brigade, 101st Airborne Division.**
Activated at Fort Campbell, Kentucky.

1967   Deployed with the **101st Airborne Division** to the Republic of Vietnam.
Vietnam Campaign Participation included the **Tet Offensive; Counteroffensive Phases III, IV, V, VI** and **VII; Tet 69/Counteroffensive; Summer-Fall 1969; Winter-Spring 1970; Sanctuary Counteroffensive;** and **Consolidations I** and **II.**

1969   Reorganized and redesignated as **HHC, 3d Brigade, 101st Airborne Division (Airmobile).**

1970   Republic of Vietnam **Cross of Gallantry with Palm**, with Streamer embroidered **VIETNAM 1968-1969**, awarded to **HHC, 3d Brigade, 101st Airborne Division.**

1971   **Valorous Unit Award**, with Streamer embroidered **THUA THIEN PROVINCE**, awarded to **HHC, 3d Brigade, 101st Airborne Division.**

Republic of Vietnam **Civic Action Honor Medal, First Class,** with Streamer embroidered **VIETNAM 1968-1970**, awarded to **HHC, 3d Brigade, 101st Airborne Division.**

1972   **Presidential Unit Citation (Army)**, with Streamer embroidered **DONG AP BIA MOUN-TAIN**, awarded to **HHC, 3d Brigade, 101st Airborne Division**
Redeployed with the **101st Airborne Division** to Fort Campbell, Kentucky.

1974   Republic of Vietnam **Cross of Gallantry with Palm**, with Streamer embroidered **VIETNAM 1971**, awarded to the **101st Airborne Division.**
Redesignated as **HHC, 3d Brigade, 101st Airborne Division (Air Assault).**

1976   **Meritorious Unit Commendation (Army)**, with Streamer embroidered **VIETNAM 1968**. awarded to **HHC, 3d Brigade, 101st Airborne Division.**

HQ, 108th Airborne Division

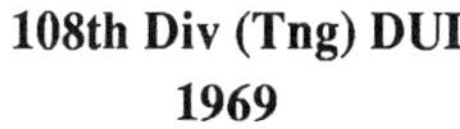

108th Div (Tng) DUI
1969

108th Abn Div SSI

1946	Constituted in the Organized Reserves as **HQ, 108th Airborne Division.** Assigned to the **Seventh Army.** Activated at Atlanta, Georgia. Relieved of assignment to **Seventh Army.** Assigned to **Third Army.**
1952	Reorganized and redesignated as **HQ, 108th Infantry Division.** Relocated to Charlotte, North Carolina.
1959	Reorganized and redesignated as **HHC, 108th Division (Training).**
1973	Relieved from assignement to **Third US Army.** Assigned to **First US Army.**
1983	Relieved from assignment to **First US Army.** Assigned to **Second US Army.**

NOTE: The DUI of the **108th Division (Training),**
was approved on 29 November 1969

Third US Army SSI

HHD, 1st Brigade, 108th Division (Training)

(HQ Company, 108th Airborne Division)

108th Div (Tng) DUI
1969

108th Airborne Div SSI

1946	Constituted in the Organized Reserves as **HQ Company, 108th Airborne Division.** Activated at Atlanta, Georgia.
1952	Reorganized and redesignated as **HQ Company, 108th Infantry Division.** Relocated to Charlotte, North Carolina.
1959	Disbanded at Charlotte, North Carolina.
1967	Reconstituted in the Army Reserve as **HHD, 1st Brigade, 108th Division (Training).**
1968	Activated at Clemson, South Carolina.

First US Army SSI

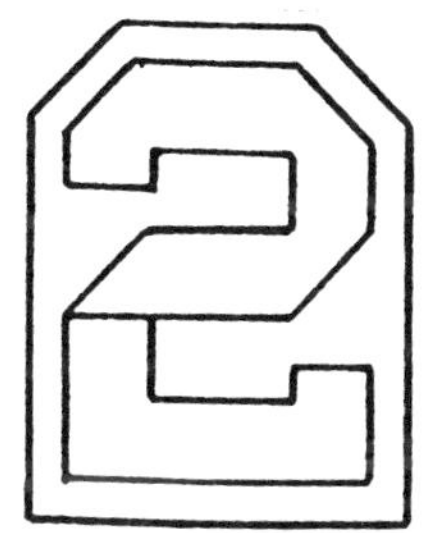

Second US Army SSI

HHD, 2d Brigade,
108th Division (Training)
(506th Airborne Field Artillery Battalion)

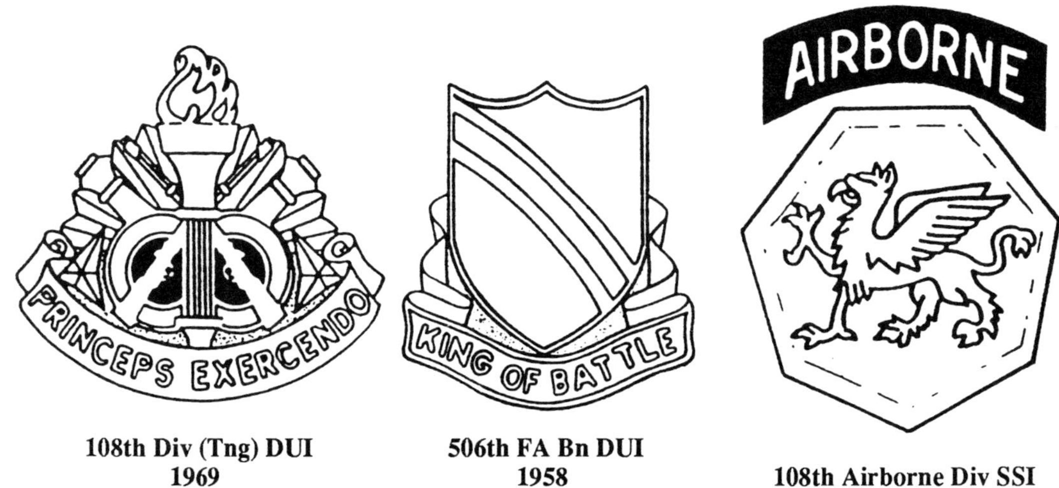

108th Div (Tng) DUI
1969

506th FA Bn DUI
1958

108th Airborne Div SSI

1946	Constituted in the Organized Reserves as the **506th Parachute Field Artillery Battalion**. Assigned to the **108th Airborne Division**. Activated at Charlotte, North Carolina.
1951	Redesignated as the **506th Airborne Field Artillery Battalion**.
1952	Reorganized and redesignated as the **506th Field Artillery Battalion**. Assigned to the **108th Infantry Division**. Relocated to Durham, North Carolina.
1959	Disbanded at Durham, North Carolina.
1967	**HHB, 506th Field Artillery Battalion** reconstituted in the Army Reserves as **HHD, 2d Brigade, 108th Division (Training)**.
1968	Activated at Hickory, North Carolina.

NOTES: 1. The DUI of the **108th Division (Training)** was authorized on 10 July 1969.
        2. The DUI of the **506th FA Battalion** was authorized on 30 January 1958.

HHD, 3d Brigade,
108th Division (Training)

108th Div (Tng) DUI	108th Airborne Div SSI

1942 — Constituted in the AUS as the **2d Battalion, 48th Engineers.**
Activated at Camp Gruber, Oklahoma.
Redesignated as the **2d Battalion, 48th Engineer Combat Regiment.**

1943 — Reorganized and redesignated as the **235th Engineer Combat Battalion.**

World War II Campaigns Participation included **Naples-Foggia, Rome-Arno, North Apennines** and **Po Valley.**

1944 — **Presidential Unit Citation (Army)**, with Streamer embroidered **MOUNT PORCHIA**, awarded to the **235th Engineer Combat Battalion.**

1946 — Inactivated in the Philippine Islands.

1952 — Allotted to the Organized Reserves, activated at Raleigh, North Carolina.
Assigned to the **108th Infantry Division.**

1953 — Inactivated at Raleigh, North Carolina.

1955 — Redesignated as the **235th Engineer Battalion**, activated at Asheboro, North Carolina.

1959 — Disbanded, (less Companies A and B, which hereafter follow a separate lineage).

1967 — **HHSC, 235th Engr Bn** reconstituted in the Army Reserve, as **HHD, 3d Bde, 108th Div (Tng).**

1968 — Activated at Charlotte, North Carolina.

1971 — Reorganized and redesignated as **HHC, 3d Brigade, 108th Division (Training).**

1978 — Reorganized and redesignated as **HHD, 3d Brigade, 108th Division (Training).**
Relocated to Winston-Salem, North Carolina.

HHD, 4th Brigade, 108th Division (Training)
(808th Airborne Ordnance Maintenance Co)

108th Div (Tng) DUI
1969

108th Airborne Div SSI

1946	Constituted in the Organized Reserves as the **808th Airborne Ordnance Maintenance Company.** Assigned to the **108th Airborne Division.** Activated at Atlanta, Georgia.
1952	Reorganized and redesignated as the **808th Ordnance Maintenance Company** Assigned to the **108th Infantry Division.** Relocated to Charlotte, North Carolina. Reorganized and redesignated as the **808th Ordnance Battalion.**
1959	Disbanded at Charlotte, North Carolina.
1967	**HHD, 808th Ordnance Battalion** reconstituted in the Army Reserve. Redesignated as **HHD, 4th Brigade, 108th Division (Training).**
1968	Activated at Raleigh, North Carolina.
1979	Relocated to Garner, North Carolina.

Phantom Airborne Divisions

9th US Airborne Division

6th US Airborne Division

18th US Airborne Division

21st US Airborne Division

135th US Airborne Division

Operation **FORTITUDE** was the largest and most successful deception plan executed during the Second World War. Operation **FORTITUDE** consisted of two elements - Operation **SKYE**, the northern (British) element; and Operation **QUICKSILVER**, the southern (US) element. A 300,000 strong ficticious allied force was reportedly preparing for the Allied invasion into Norway and the Pas-de-Calais area of France. Twenty of the non-existant allied divisions came from the United States, with five designated as airborne divisions. The meticulous planning for this important psychological misinformation, included the issuance of orders and phoney message traffic, also the normal design approval process and manufacture of shoulder sleeve insignia. The designs of the SSI for the **6th, 9th, 18th, 21st** and **135th Airborne Divisions** of the US contingent, are shown above. The actual invasion, as history reveals, was successfully accomplished into Normandy, France. Although never activated, the elements of Operation **FORTITUDE** played a significant role during World War II. The **108th Airborne Division,** activated after WW II, was originally listed as a conventional Infantry Division during Operation **QUICKSILVER.**

COLOR ILLUSTRATIONS

Color illustrations of the Airborne Headquarters and Commands insignia may be found in pages 65 through 72. Illustrations are generally grouped in the following categories:

Organization	SSI	DUI	Flash/Oval
Army Headquarters SSI	65		
Airborne Command	65		70
Corps Headquarters	66	68	71
Corps Artillery		65	
Corps Support Command	66	68	71
IX Engineer Command	66		
Abn Troop Carrier Cmd	66		
Airborne Divisions	66-67	65, 68	70
Cavalry Division	72	68	70
Infantry Divisions	67	68	
Training Divisions		68	
Airborne Brigades	72	68, 69	70, 71
Artillery Battalions		69	
Engr Battalions		69	
Ordnance Companies		68	

NOTE: Within the index of this volume, illustrations are indicated by page numbers in bold print and enclosed by parenthesis. For example:

AIRBORNE
 <u>**DIVISIONS**</u>

82d Airborne Div   (iii), 4, 5, 6, 8, 12, 15-16, 17, 30-38,73, 74, 76, 90, **(67, 68, 70)**

HHC, 82d Airborne Div   30-31,

HQ, 82d Airborne Div   30-38

HQ Troop, 82d Airborne Div 32

Command and Control Bn   33

1st Brigade   32, 33,

HHC, 1st Brigade   32, 33, **(70)**

Color illustrations in the above example are on pages 67, 68 and 70.

First US Army SSI

Second US Army SSI

Third US Army SSI

Fourth US Army SSI

Fifth US Army SSI

US Airborne Cmd SSI

11th Airborne Div
(Cmd & Control Bn
(Unauth DUI)

XVIII Corps Arty DUI

First Allied Abn Army SSI
1944-1945

First US Airborne Army (1945 variations)

1st Abn Task Force
(Unauth cap insignia)

XVIII Corps SSI
1943-44

XVIII Corps (Abn) SSI
XVIII Abn Corps SSI
1944

1st COSCOM SSI
(Abn Tab worn by
airborne duty personnel)

6th Airborne Div SSI

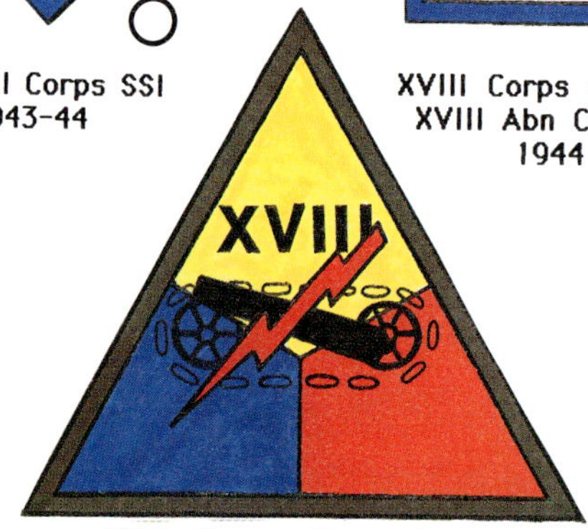

XVIII Corps (Unauth) SSI
1943

18th Airborne Div SSI

1st Troop Carrier
Cmd SSI (Unauth)

11th Airborne Div SSI
1942-1958

11th Air Assault Div
SSI 1963-1965

IX Engr Cmd SSI

Abn Troop Carrier Cmd

13th Airborne Div SSI

17th Airborne Div SSI

9th Airborne Div SSI

21st Airborne Div SSI

80th Airborne Div SSI

82d Airborne Div SSI

84th Airborne Div SSI

100th Airborne Div SSI

101st Abn Div SSI

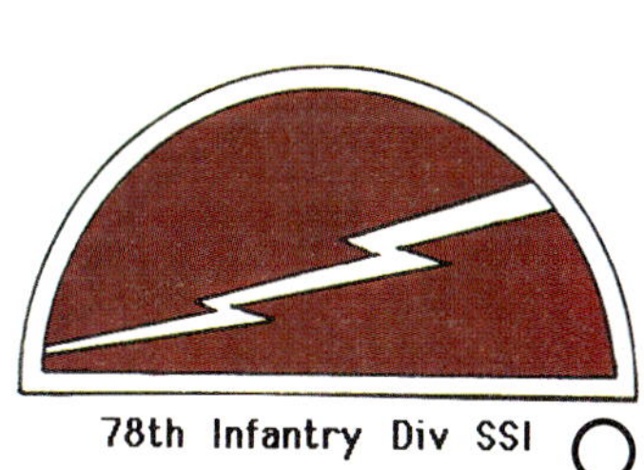

78th Infantry Div SSI

1st Infantry Div SSI

108th Airborne Div SSI

135th Airborne Div SSI

1st COSCOM DUI   1st Cavalry Div DUI   8th Infantry Div DUI   24th Infantry Div DUI

80th Div (Tng) DUI   82d Airborne Div DUI   84th Div (Tng) DUI   100th Div (Tng) DUI

101st Abn Div DUI   101st Airborne Div DUI   108th Div (Tng) DUI   173d Airborne Bde DUI

XVIII Abn Corps (pre 1987)   XVIII Abn Corps DUI 1987   784th Ord Bn DUI   800th Abn OD Mt Co (Unauth)

16th MP Bde DUI

18th Avn Bde DUI

18th FA Bde DUI

20th Engr Bde DUI

35th Signal Bde DUI

71st Airborne Bde DUI

82d Avn Bde DUI

101st Avn Bde DUI

525th MI Bde DUI

305th Engr Bn DUI

309th Abn Engr Bn DUI

325th Engr Bn DUI

506th FA Bn DUI

905th FA Bn DUI

909th FA Bn DUI

925th Abn FA Bn DUI

HQ, 82d Airborne Div
Abn Oval and Flash

1st Bde, 82d Abn Div
Abn Oval and Flash

2d Bde, 82d Abn Div
Abn Oval and Flash

3d Bde, 82d Abn Div
Abn Oval and Flash

4th Bde, 82d Abn Div
Abn Oval

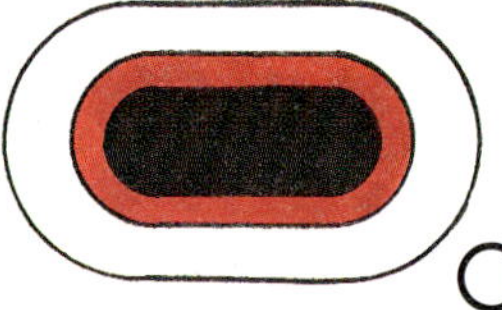

US Airborne Command
Airborne Oval

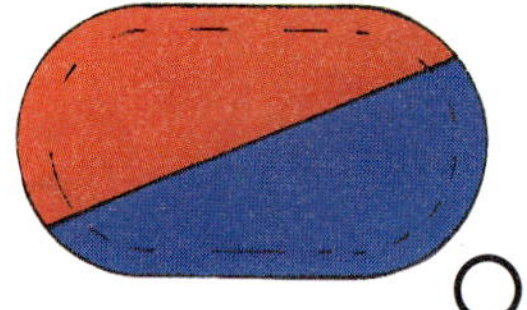

173d Airborne Bde
Abn Oval

173d Airborne Bde
(RVN made Abn Oval)

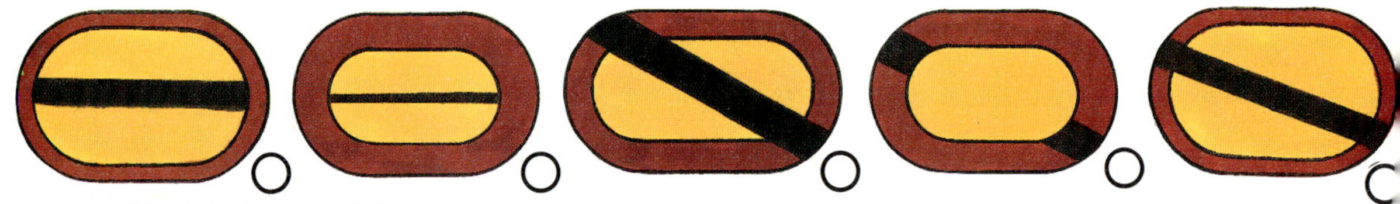

HQ, 1st Cavalry Division
(Unauth RVN made Abn Ovals)

1st Bde, 1st Cavalry Division
(Unauth RVN made Abn Oval variations)

HQ, 101st Airborne Div
Airborne Oval
Airmobile Flash

1st Bde, 101st Abn Div
Airborne Oval
Airmobile Flash

2d Bde, 101st Abn Div
Airborne Oval
Airmobile Flash

3d Bde, 101st Abn Div
Airborne Oval
Airmobile Flash

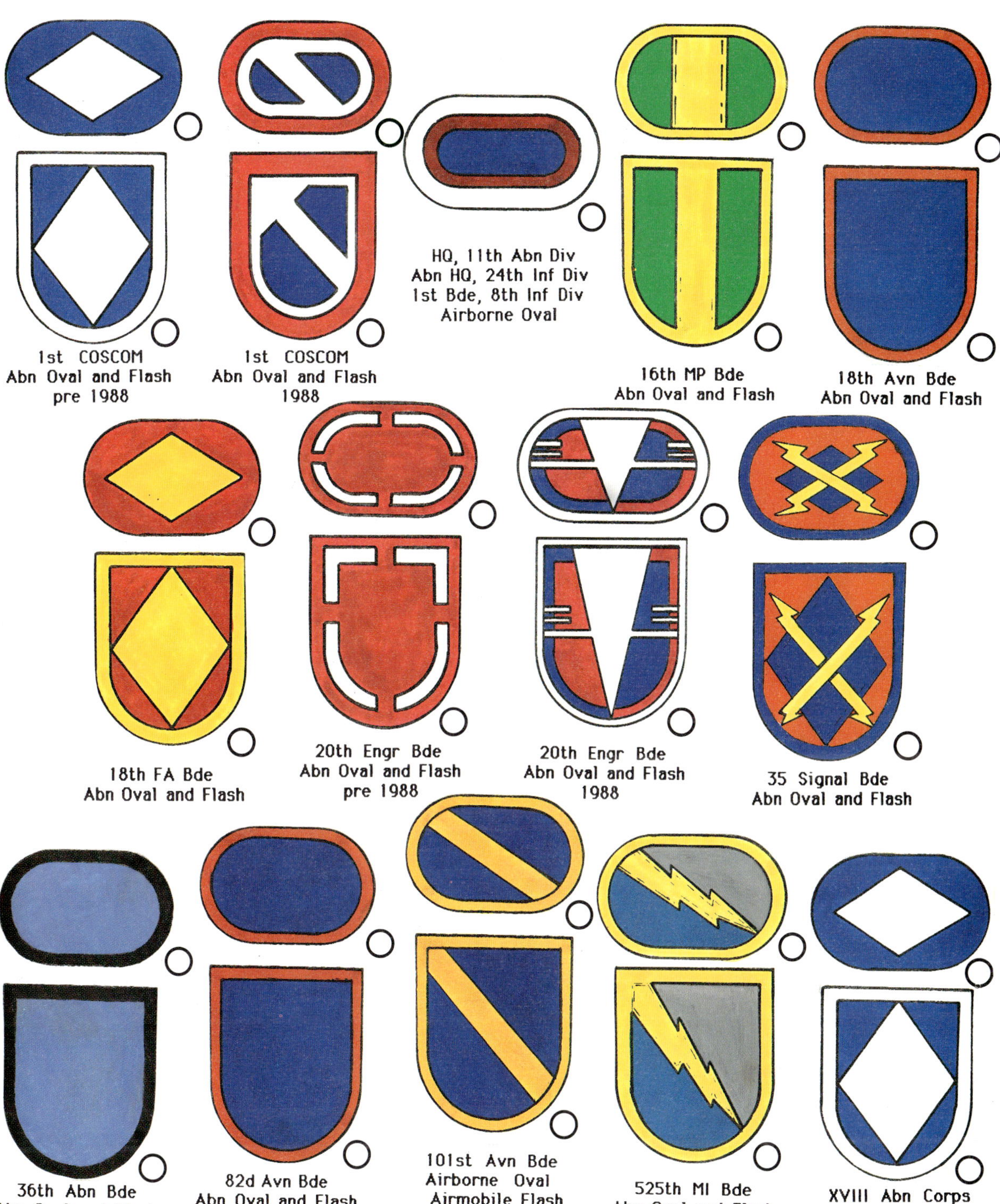

1st COSCOM
Abn Oval and Flash
pre 1988

1st COSCOM
Abn Oval and Flash
1988

HQ, 11th Abn Div
Abn HQ, 24th Inf Div
1st Bde, 8th Inf Div
Airborne Oval

16th MP Bde
Abn Oval and Flash

18th Avn Bde
Abn Oval and Flash

18th FA Bde
Abn Oval and Flash

20th Engr Bde
Abn Oval and Flash
pre 1988

20th Engr Bde
Abn Oval and Flash
1988

35 Signal Bde
Abn Oval and Flash

36th Abn Bde
Abn Oval and Flash

82d Avn Bde
Abn Oval and Flash

101st Avn Bde
Airborne Oval
Airmobile Flash

525th MI Bde
Abn Oval and Flash

XVIII Abn Corps
Abn Oval and Flash

20th Engr Bde SSI

1st Bde, 8th Inf Div SSI

Abn HQ, 24th Inf Div SSI

525th MI Bde SSI

2d Abn Inf Bde SSI

18th Avn Bde SSI

36th/71st Abn Bde SSI

18th FA Bde SSI

173d Abn Bde SSI

16th MP Bde SSI

1st Bde, 1st Cav Div (Airmobile) SSI

35th Signal Bde SSI

Chapter Five

US Army Airborne Brigades

The first two separate airborne brigades in the US Army were the **1st** and **2d Airborne Infantry Brigades**, both with lineages from the **1st Infantry Division**. The **1st Airborne Infantry Brigade** assigned to the **Airborne Command** at Camp Mackall, North Carolina, was tasked with training and preparing airborne units for their combat missions. The **2d Airborne Infantry Brigade** deployed from Camp Mackall to the ETO, with the **501st** and **508th Parachute Infantry Regiments** assigned. **The 2d Airborne Brigade** was not employed as a combat command. The **501st** was attached to the **101st Airborne Division** and the **508th** to the **82d Airborne Division** for the Normandy landings, and remained so attached until the end of the war.

As the **11th Airborne Division** prepared to inactivate in Germany in 1958, the **24th Infantry Division**, was reconfigured to continue the many airborne missions performed by the **11th Airborne Division** In 1959, these same functions were assumed by the **8th Infantry Division.** For several months in 1958, prior to the **8th Infantry Division** assuming these airborne functions, an airborne headquarters was established by the **24th Infantry Division**. The airborne elements of the **24th Infantry Division** were the **1st Airborne Battle Groups** of the 187th and **503d Infantry**, and the **11th QM Supply and Parachute Maintenance Company**. The **1st Airborne Battle Group, 187th Infantry** developed an airborne tab with red letters on a black background, other airborne elements within the **24th Infantry Division** wore the black airborne tab with gold letters. The **1st Brigade (Abn), 8th Infantry Division** was activated in 1963, providing an airborne headquarters for the next decade. In 1973, the **1st Battalion, 509th Airborne Infantry** was reassigned from the 1st Brigade, 8th Infantry Division, to continue airborne commitments in Vincenza, Italy; the **2d Battalion** was inactivated, and the **3d Battalion** reverted back to reasignment as **Company C, 509th Infantry.** Airborne infantry regiments and their battalions are included in Volume 3 of this series - __A Concise History of US Army Airborne Infantry.__

From 1963-1965, the **11th Airborne Division** was reorganized and activated as the **11th Air Assault Division** at Fort Benning, Georgia. The resounding success of the airmobile concepts as demonstrated by the **11th Air Assault Division**, paved the way for the reorganization of the **1st Cavalry Division (Airmobile)** in 1965. The **1st Brigade, 1st Cavalry Division** was organized as an airborne brigade as the Division deployed to South Vietnam in 1965, until their airborne capability was discontinued in 1966.

Other early deployers to South Vietnam, and both functioning as separate airborne brigades were the **173d Airborne Brigade** and the **1st Brigade, 101st Airborne Division.,** The **173d** remained in an airborne role as a separate brigade, until returning to Fort Campbell, Kentucky, where it's assets were absorbed into the **101st Airborne Division (Airmobile)** The **1st Brigade, 101st Airborne Division** relinquished it's separate brigade status with the arrival of the remainbder of the **101st Airborne Division** into the Republic of Vietnam in 1967.

The only airborne brigade in the reserve component of the US Army was the **36th Airborne Brigade**, assigned to the Texas Army National Guard (ARNG). The sames rules for lineage complexity appear to apply as equally to the ARNG as they do to the active component. In January 1968, **HQ, 71st Infantry Brigade** was organized from consolidating **HHC, 1st Battalion, 36th Infantry Division** with **HHC and Company B, 7th Battalion, 112th Armor Regiment.** On 1 November 1971, **HQ Company, 71st Infantry Brigade** was reorganized and redesignated as **HQ Company, 71st Airborne Brigade.** In 1973 until inactivated in 1980, the **71st Airborne Brigade** was redesignated as the **36th Airborne Brigade. HHC, 36th Airborne Brigade** was reorganized and redesignated as **HHC, 386th Engineer Battalion** in 1980.

Five major elements of the **XVIII Airborne Corps** have been elevated to Brigade status during the past decade. The **XVIII Airborne Corps Artillery** (constituted in 1943), was redesignated as the **18th Field Artillery**

Brigade. Also constituted in 1943, the **931st Signal Battalion**, which transitioned to become the **35th Signal Group**, became the **35th Signal Brigade** in 1979.

The **16th Military Police Group** and the **525th Military Intelligence Group** were both constituted and activated in 1946. The **16th Military Police Brigade** was designated in 1981 and the **525th Military Intelligence Group** became a brigade in 1985. The **525th Military Intelligence Brigade** was the first combat electronic warfare intelligence brigade in the US Army.

The **269th Aviation Battalion**, constituted in 1966, became the **18th Aviation Brigade** in 1987. At the time of writing, the **18th Aviation Brigade** and the **82d Aviation Brigade**, at Fort Bragg, North Carolina, are both wearing the same design and color oval wing background and beret flash. Also included in this volume are the Aviation Brigades of the **82d Airborne Division** and the **101st Airborne Division (Air Assault)**.The oval wing background of the **Aviation Brigade** of the **101st Airborne Division** is still authorized, being officially recognized by the Department of the Army Institute of Heraldry on 29 February 1988. The DUI (authorized for the **101st Aviation Group** in October 1969), was authorized for wear by the Aviation Brigade on 3 April 1986. The flash was worn when blue berets were worn by the **101st Airborne Division (Airmobile),** at Fort Campbell, Kentucky when they returned to that location from Vietnam in an airmobile status. The blue and gold aviation beret flash (also Chemical Corps colors), was later adopted by the **445th Chemical Detachment (NBC Recon) (Special Forces)**, at Columbus, Georgia (see **Volume 1, <u>A Concise History of US Army Special Operations Forces)</u>.**

The longest lineage of any brigade of the **XVIII Airborne Corps** belongs to the **20th Engineer Brigade**. Organized as the **Battalion of Engineers** in 1861, this unit served in the Civil War, the War with Spain, the Philippine Insurection, the Mexican Wars, World Wars I and II, and in the Republic of Vietnam. The **20th Engineer Brigade** is the only <u>airborne</u> engineer brigade in the US Army, and the only engineer brigade stationed in the Continental United States. The oval wing background and flash worn today by the **20th Engineer Brigade** was originally authorized for the **27th Engineer Battalion,** and was transferred to the **20th Engineer Brigade** during the 1988 transition to standardize ovals and flashes within the Brigade. The **37th Engineer Battalion** wears the third oval and flash combination in this series, (see **Volume 7, <u>A Concise History of US Army Airborne Combat Support)</u>.**

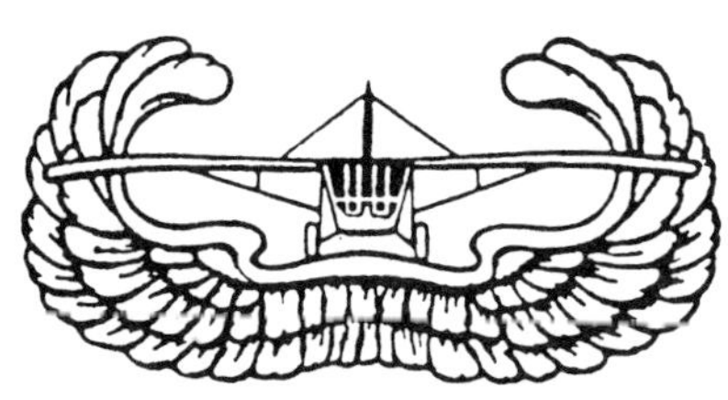

US Army Glider badge

1st Airborne Infantry Brigade

US Airborne Cmd SSI

1917	Constituted in the Regular Army as **HQ, 1st Infantry Brigade.**
	Assigned to the **1st Expeditionary Force,** (later the **1st Infantry Division**).
	Organized at New York City, New York.
	World War I Campaign Participation included **Montdidier-Noyon; Aisne-Marne; St Mihiel; Meusse-Argonne; Lorraine 1917; Lorraine 1918** and **Picardy 1918.**
1921	Reorganized and redesignated as **HHC, 1st Infantry Brigade.**
1925	Redesignated as **HHC, 1st Brigade.**
1936	Redesignated as **HHC, 1st Infantry Brigade.**
1939	Disbanded at Camp Wadsworth, New York.
1943	Reconstituted in the Regular Army as <u>**HHC, 1st Airborne Brigade.**</u>
	Activated at Camp Meade, South Dakota.
	Assigned to the **US Airborne Command.**
	Relocated to Camp Mackall, North Carolina.
1944	Disbanded at Camp Mackall, North Carolina.
1958	Reconstituted in the Regular Army as **HHC, 1st Infantry Brigade.**
	Activated at Fort Benning, Georgia.
1962	Inactivated at Fort Benning, Georgia.
1963	Redesignated as **HHC, 1st Brigade, 1st Infantry Division.**
1964	Activated at Fort Riley, Kansas.
	Vietnam Campaign Participation included the **Defense; Counteroffensive; Counteroffensive Phases II, III, IV, V and VI; Tet Counteroffensive; Tet 69/Counteroffensive; Summer-Fall 1969** and **Winter-Spring 1970.**
1969	Republic of Vietnam **Cross of Gallantry with Palm,** with Streamer embroidered **VIETNAM 1965-1968,** awarded to **HHC, 1st Brigade, 1st Infantry Division.**
1970	Republic of Vietnam **Civic Action Honor Medal, First Class,** with Streamer embroidered **VIETNAM 1965-1970,** awarded to HHC, 1st Brigade, 1st Infantry Division.
1971	Republic of Vietnam **Cross of Gallantry with Palm,** with Streamer embroidered **VIETNAM 1969-1970,** awarded to HHC, 1st Brigade, 1st Infantry Division.

2d Airborne Infantry Brigade

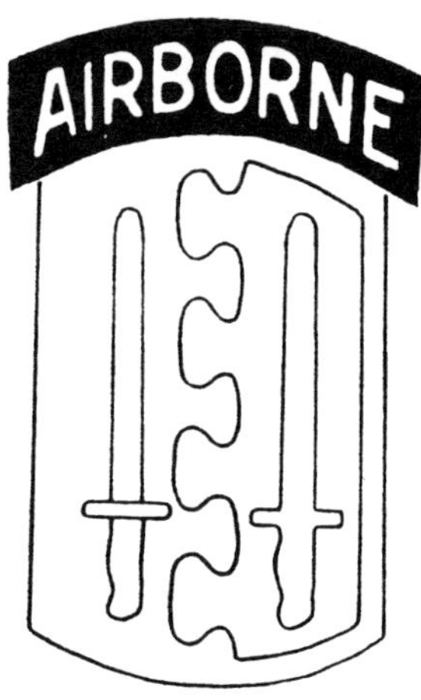

2d Abn Inf Bde SSI

1917	Constituted in the Regular Army as **HQ, 2d Infantry Brigade.**
	Assigned to the **1st Expeditionary Force**, (later designated as the **1st Division**).
	Organized at New York City, New York.
	World War I Campaign Participation included **Montdidier-Noyon; Aisne-Marne; St Mihiel; Meusse-Argonne; Lorraine 1917; Lorraine 1918** and **Picardy 1918.**
1921	Reorganized and redesignated as **HHC, 2d Infantry Brigade.**
1925	Redesignated as **HHC, 2d Brigade.**
1936	Redesignated as **HHC, 2d Infantry Brigade.**
1939	Relieved from assignment to the **1st Division.**
1940	Inactivated at Fort Ontario, New York.
1943	Redesignated as __HHC, 2d Airborne Infantry Brigade,__ activated at Camp Mackall, North Carolina.
	WorldWar II Campaign Participation included **Normandy.**
	(The assigned **501st** and **508th Parachute Infantry Regiments**, were attached to the **82d** and **101st Airborne Divisions**).
1945	Disbanded in England.
1958	Reconstituted in the Regular Army as **HHC, 2d Infantry Brigade.**
	Activated at Fort Devens, Massachusetts.
1962	Inactivated at Fort Devens, Massachusetts.
1963	Redesignated as **HHC, 2d Brigade, 1st Infantry Division.**
	Vietnam Campaign Participation included the **Defense; Counbteroffensive; Counteroffensive Phases II, III, IV, V** and **VI; Tet Counteroffensive; Tet/69 Counteroffensive; Summer-Fall 1969** and **Winter-Spring 1970.**
1969	Republic of Vietnam **Cross of Gallantry with Palm**, with Streamer embroidered **VIETNAM 1965-1968**, awarded to **HHC, 2d Brigade, 1st Infantry Division.**
1970	Republic of Vietnam **Civic Action Honor Medal, First Class**, with Streamer embroidered **VIETNAM 1965-1970**, awarded to **HHC, 2d Brigade, 1st Infantry Division.**
1971	**Meritorious Unit Commendadtion (Army)**, with Streamer embroidered **VIETNAM 1969**, awarded to **HHC, 2d Brigade, 1st Infantry Division.**

HHC, 1st Bde (Abn),1st Cav Div

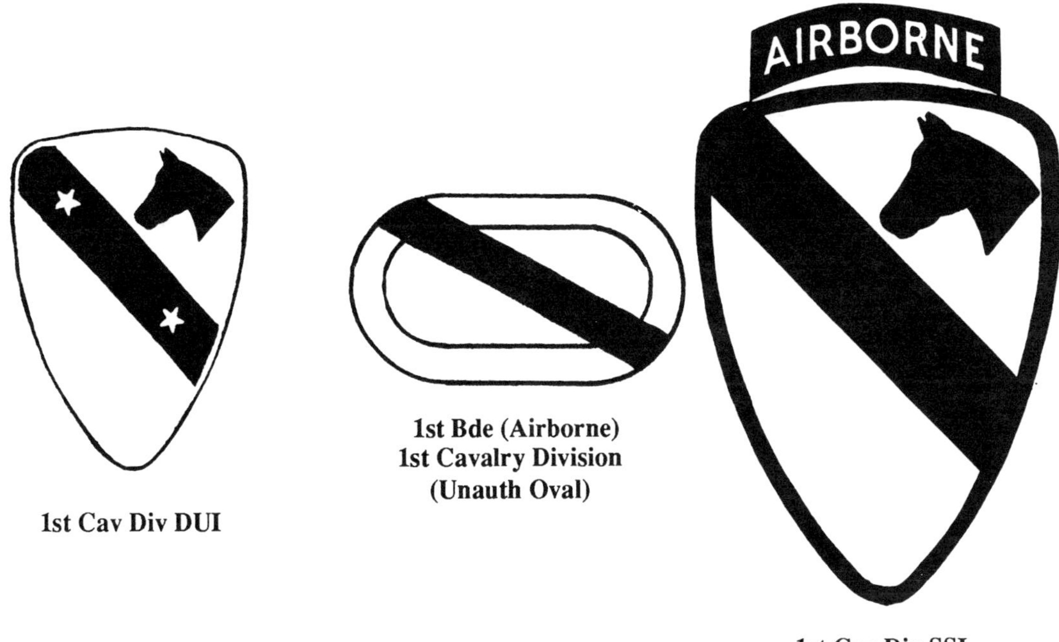

1st Cav Div DUI

1st Bde (Airborne)
1st Cavalry Division
(Unauth Oval)

1st Cav Div SSI

1917	Constituted in the Regular Army as **HQ, 1st Cavalry Brigade.**
1918	Organized at Fort Sam Houston, Texas. Assigned to the **15th Cavalry Division.** Relieved from assignment to the **15th Cavalry Division.**
1919	Demobilized at Brownsville, Texas.
1921	Reconstituted in the Regular Army as **HHT, 1st Cavalry Brigade.** Assigned to the**1st Cavalry Division.** Organized at Camp Harry J. Jones, Arizona.

World War II Campaign Participation included **New Guinea, Bismarck Archipelago** (with arrowhead), **Leyte** (with arrowhead) and **Luzon.**

1948	**Presidential Unit Citation (Army)**, with Streamer embroidered LUZON, awarded to **HHT, 1st Cavalry Brigade.**
1949	Relieved from assignment to the **1st Cavalry Division Special.** Inactivated in Japan. Converted and redesignated as **HQ, 1st Constabulary Brigade.** Assigned to the **US Constabulary.** Activated in Germany.

1950   Relieved from assignment to the **US Constabulary.**

     Philippine Presidential Unit Citation, with Streamer embroidered 17 OCTOBER 1944 TO 4 JULY 1945, awarded to **HHT, 1st Cavalry Brigade.**

1951   Inactivated in Germany.

1963   Reconstituted in the Regular Army as **HHC, 1st Brigade, 1st Cavalry Division.** Activated in Korea.

1965   Deployed with the **1st Cavalry Division** to the Republic of Vietnam. Redesignated as **HHC, 1st Brigade (Airborne), 1st Cavalry Division.**

     Vietnam Campaign Participation included **Defense; Counteroffensive; Counteroffensive Phases II, III, IV, V, VI and VII; Tet Counteroffensive; Tet 69/Counteroffensive; Summer-Fall 1969; Winter-Spring 1970** and the **Sanctuary Counteroffensive.**

1966   Redesignated as **HHC, 1st Brigade, 1st Cavalry Division.**

1967   **Presidential Unit Citation (Army), with Streamer embroidered PLEIKU**, awarded to **HHC, 1st Brigade, 1st Cavalry Division.**

1969   Republic of Vietnam **Cross of Gallantry with Palm,** with Streamer embroidered **VIETNAM 1965-1969**, awarded to **HHC, 1st Brigade, 1st Cavalry Division.**

1970   **Valorous Unit Award,** with Streamer embroidered **FISH HOOK**, awarded to **HHC, 1st Brigade, 1st Cavalry Division.**

1971   Redeployed with the **1st Cavalry Division** to Fort Hood, Texas.

1972   Republic of Vietnam **Cross of Gallantry with Palm,** with Streamer embroidered **VIETNAM 1969-1970**, awarded to **HHC, 1st Brigade, 1st Cavalry Division.**

     Republic of Vietnam **Civic Action Honor Medal First Class,** with Streamer embroidered **VIETNAM 1969-1970**, awarded to **HHC, 1st Brigade, 1st Cavalry Division.**

NOTE: There have been many variations of the **1st Cavalry Div** DUI over the years. An early version (without the two stars on the bend), was made in Japan. The bend has been colored blue and black. The DUI shown, (worn during the 1920-1930 era), was officially approved for the Division Command and Staff, and non color bearing units (NCBU) on 21 April 1966.

1st Bde (Abn), 8th Infantry Div

8th Inf Div DUI 1958

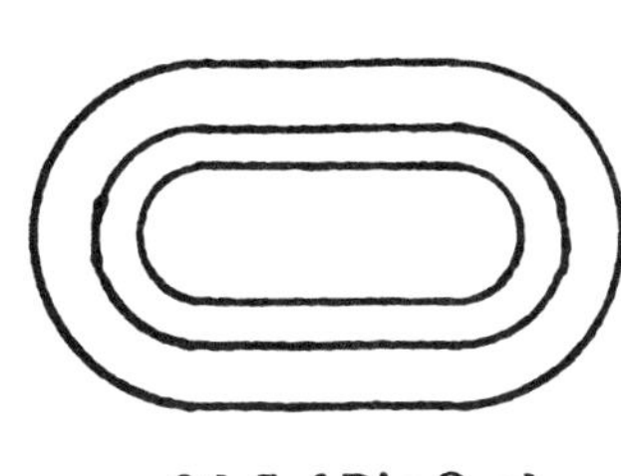

8th Inf Div Oval

1st Bde (Abn), 8th Inf Div SSI

1917	Constituted in the Regular Army as HQ Troop, 8th Division.
1918	Organized at Camp Fremont, California.
	World War I Campaign Participation provided a Streamer without inscription.
1919	Demobilized at Camp Dix, New Jersey.
1923	Reconstituted in the Regular Army as HQ and MP Co (less the MP Platoon), 8th Division.
1940	Activated at Camp Jackson, South Carolina.
1942	Redesignated as **HQ and Military Police Company (less Military Police Platoon), 8th Motorized Division.**
1943	Reorganized and redesignated as **HQ Company, 8th Infantry Division.** World War II Campaign Participation included **Normandy, Northern France, the Rhineland and Central Europe.**
1945	Inactivated at Fort Leonard Wood, Missouri.
1950	Activated at Fort Jackson, South Carolina.
1960	Disbanded in Germany.
1963	Reconstituted in the Regular Army as HHC, 1st Brigade, 8th Infantry Division. Activated in Germany. Redesignated as HHC, 1st Brigade (Airborne), 8th Infantry Division
1969	Luxembourg **Croix de Guerre**, with Streamer embroidered LUXEMBOURG, awarded to the **8th Infantry Division.**
1973	Reorganized and redesignated as HHC, 1st Brigade, 8th Infantry Div.

NOTE: As the elements of the **24th Infantry Division** assumed the airborne role and missions from the **11th Airborne Division**, they also assumed the oval wing background that was worn by the HQ, 11th Airborne Division. This same wing background was passed on to the 1st Brigade (Airborne), 8th Infantry Division when they assumed the same airborne mission command and control responsibilities from 1963 to 1973.

HHC, 16th Military Police Bde (Abn)

16th MP Brigade DUI

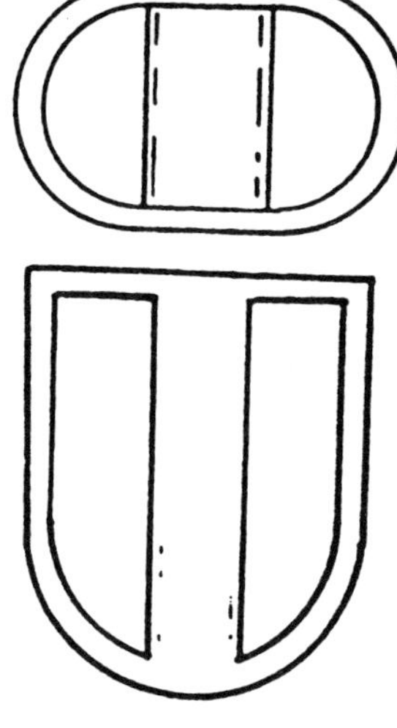

16th MP Brigade
Oval and Flash

16th MP Brigade SSI

1966	Constituted in the Regular Army as **HHD, 16th Military Police Group.** Activated at Fort George G. Meade, Maryland.
	Deployed to the Republic of Vietnam.
	Vietnam Campaign Participation included Counteroffensive Phases II, III, IV, V, VI and VII; Tet Counteroffensive; Tet 69/Counteroffensive; Winter-Spring 1970; the Sanctuary Counteroffensive; and Consolidations I and II.
1969	Meritorious Unit Commendation (Army), with Streamer embroidered **VIETNAM 1966-1968**, awarded to HHD, 16th Military Police Group.
1970	Meritorious Unit Commendation (Army), with Streamer embroidered **VIENAM 1968-1969**, awarded to HHD, 16th Military Police Group.
1972	Republic of Vietnam **Cross of Gallantry with Palm**, with Streamer embroidered **VIETNAM 1966-1971**, awarded to the **16th Military Police Group.**
1981	Reorganized and redesignated as HHC, 16th Military Police Brigade.

HHC, 18th Aviation Brigade (Abn)

18th Aviation Bde DUI

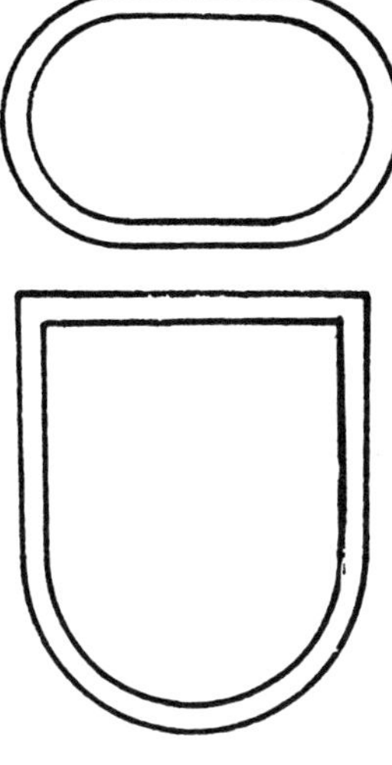

**18th Aviation Bde
Oval and Flash**

18th Aviation Bde SSI

1966	Constituted in the Regular Army as **HHD, 269th Aviation Battalion.** Activated at Fort Bragg, North Carolina.
1968	**Meritorious Unit Commendation (Army),** with Streamer embroidered **VIETNAM 1967,** awarded to **HHD, 269th Aviation Battalion.**
	Republic of Vietnam **Cross of Gallantry with Palm,** with Streamer embroidered **VIETNAM 1967-1967,** awarded to **HHD, 269th Aviation Battalion.** Reorganized and redesignated as **HHC, 269th Aviation Battalion.**
1969	Republic of Vietnam **Cross of Gallantry with Palm,** with Streamer embroidered **VIETNAM 1967-1968,** awarded to **HHD, 269th Aviation Battalion.**
1970	Republic of Vietnam **Cross of Gallantry with Palm,** with Streamer embroidered **VIETNAM 1968,** awarded to **HHD, 269th Aviation Battalion.**
1971	Republic of Vietnam **Civic Action Honor Medal, First Class,** with Streamer embroidered **VIETNAM 1967-1970,** awarded to **HHC, 269th Aviation Bn.**
1972	Republic of Vietnam **Cross of Gallantry with Palm,** with Streamer embroidered **VIETNAM 1968-1970,** awarded to **HHC, 269th Aviation Battalion.**
	Republic of Vietnam **Civic Action Honor Medal, First Class,** with Streamer embroidered **VIETNAM 1970,** awarded to **HHC, 269th Aviation Battalion.**
1987	Reorganized and redesignated as **HHC, 18th Aviation Brigade.** Assigned to the **XVIII Airborne Corps.**

HHB, 18th Field Artillery Brigade (Airborne)

18th FA Brigade DUI

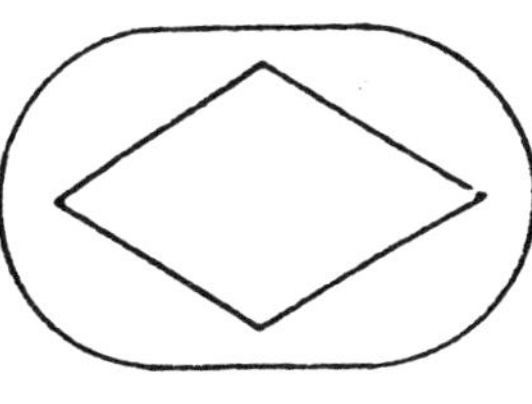

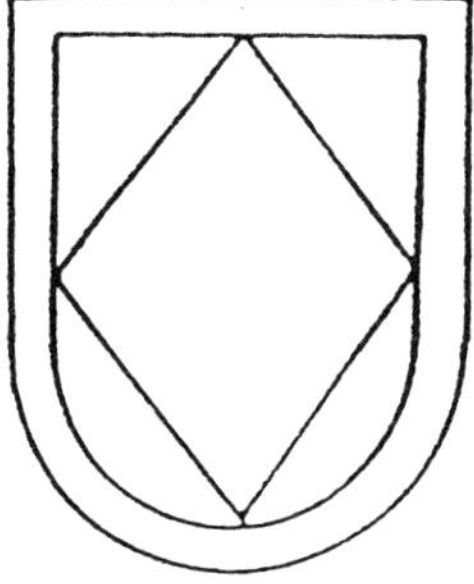

**18th FA Brigade
Oval and Flash**

**18th FA Brigade SSI
(Auth Oct 1987)**

1943	Constituted in the AUS as **HHB, XVIII Corps Artillery.** Activated at Camp Cooke, California. World War II Campaign Participation included the **Rhineland; Ardennes-Alsace** and **Central Europe.**
1945	Inactivated at Camp Campbell, Kentucky.
1951	Redesignated as **HHB, XVIII Airborne Corps Artillery.** Allotted to the Regular Army. Activated at Fort Bragg, North Carolina.
1978	Reorganized and redesignated as **HHB, 18th Field Artillery Brigade.**

XVIII Corps Artillery DUI

HHC, 20th Engineer Brigade (Abn)

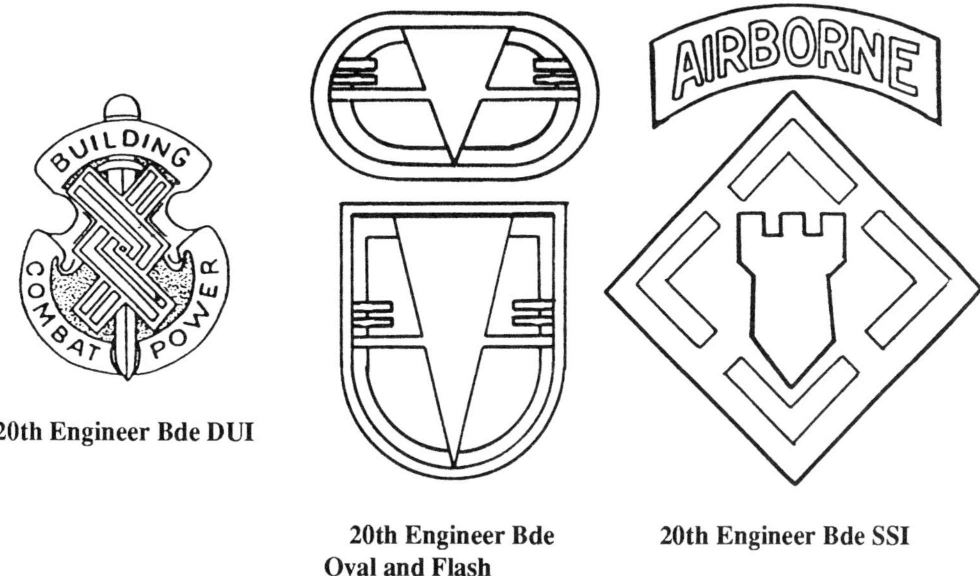

20th Engineer Bde DUI

20th Engineer Bde
Oval and Flash
1988

20th Engineer Bde SSI

1861	Organized in the Regular Army at Washington DC, from existing companies, as the **Battalion of Engineer Troops.**
	Civil War Campaign Participation included the **Peninsular; Antietam; Fredericksburg, Chancellorsville; Wilderness; Spotsylvania; Cold Harbor; Petersburg; Appomattox** and **Virginia 1863.**
1866	**Battalion of Engineer Troops** redesignated as the **Battalion of Engineers.**
1901	Expanded (14 March - 7 June), to form the **1st Battalion of Engineers** (hereafter following a separate lineage); and the **2d Battalion of Engineers.**
	War with Spain Campaign Participation included **Santiago.**
	Philippine Insurrection Campaign Participation included **Tarlac;Mindanao.**
1916	**2d Battalion of Engineers** expanded (1 July - 1 August), to form the **2d Regiment of Engineers.**
	Mexican Expedition Campaign Participation included **Mexico 1916-1917.**
1917	**2d Regiment of Engineers** expanded (21 May - 20 June), as shown:

    Companies A and **B** (and part of the Headquarters expanded in 1917), consolidated to form the **2d Regiment of Engineers** (hereafter following a separate lineage).

    Company C reorganized and redesignated as **Company C, 2d Regiment of Engineers** (hereafter following a separate lineage).

    Company D, organized 1916 at Ojo Federico, Mexico, consolidated with part of the Headquarters expanded in 1917, to form the **5th Regiment of Engineers.**

<u>Companies E</u> and <u>F</u> (and part of the Headquarters expanded in 1917), consolidated to form the **4th Regiment of Engineers**, (hereafter following a separate lineage).

5th Regiment of Engineers redesignated as the **5th Engineers.**
Assigned to the **7th Division.**

World War I Campaign Participation included **Lorraine 1918.**

1921 Inactivated at Camp Humpries, Virginia.

1936 Relieved from assignment to the **7th Division.**
Activated at Fort Belvoir, Virginia.

1942 Redesignated as the **5th Engineer Combat Regiment.**

1943 Elements of the **5th Engineer Combat Regiment** reorganized and redesignated as shown:

  HHSC, 5th Engineer Combat Regiment redesignated as **HHC, 1128th Engineer Combat Group.**
  1st and **2d Battalions, 5th Engineer Combat Regiment** redesignated as the **1277th** and the **1278th Engineer Combat Battalions** respectively (and hereafter following a separate lineage).

World War II Campaign Participation included **Normandy; Northern France; Rhineland; Ardennes-Alsace** and **Central Europe.**

1946 **HHC, 1128th Engineer Combat Group** inactivated in Germany.

1950 Redesignated as **HHC, 20th Engineer Brigade.**
Activated at Fort Leonard Wood, Missouri.

1958 Inactivated at Fort Bragg, North Carolina.

1967 Activated at Fort Bragg, North Carolina.
Deployed to the Republic of Vietnam.

Vietnam Campaign Participation included **Tet Counteroffensive; Counteroffensive Phases III, IV, V, VI** and **VII; Tet 69/Counteroffensive; Summer- Fall 1969; Winter-Spring 1970; Sactuary Counteroffensive** and **Consolidation I.**

1969 **Meritorious Unit Commendation (Army),** with Streamer embroidered **VIETNAM 1967-1968,** awarded to **HHC, 20th Engineer Brigade.**

Meritorious Unit Commendation (Army), with Streamer embroidered **VIETNAM 1968,** awarded to **HHC, 20th Engineer Brigade.**

1971 **Meritorious Unit Commendation (Army),** with Streamer embroidered **VIETNAM 1968-1970,** awarded to **HHC, 20th Engineer Brigade.**

Meritorious Unit Commendation (Army), with Streamer embroidered **VIETNAM 1970-1971,** awarded to **HHC, 20th Engineer Brigade.**

Republic of Vietnam **Civic Action Honor Medal, First Class,** with Streamer embroidered **VIETNAM 1967-1970,** awarded to **HHC, 20th Engineer Brigade.**
Inactivated in the Republic of Vietnam.

1974 Activated at Fort Bragg, North Carolina.
Assigned to the **XVIII Airborne Corps.**

HHC, 35th Signal Brigade (Abn)

35th Signal Bde DUI

35th Signal Bde
Oval and Flash

35th Signal Bde SSI

1943	Constituted in the AUS as the **931st Signal Battalion (Air Support Command)**. Activated at Esler, Louisiana.
	World War II Campaign Participation included **Central Burma; India-Burma** and the **China Offensive.**
	Meritorious Unit Commendation (Army), with Streamer embroidered **ASIATIC-PACIFIC THEATER**, awarded to the **931st Signal Battalion.**
1945	Inactivated in India.
1967	**HHC, 931st Signal Battalion** redesignated as **HHD, 35th Signal Group**. Allotted to the Regular Army. Assigned to **XVIII Airborne Corps**. Activated at Fort Bragg, North Carolina.
1979	Reorganized and redesignated as **HHC, 35th Signal Brigade (Corps) (Airborne)**. Assigned to **US Army Forces Command** and **XVIII Airborne Corps.**

36th Airborne Brigade (TXARNG)

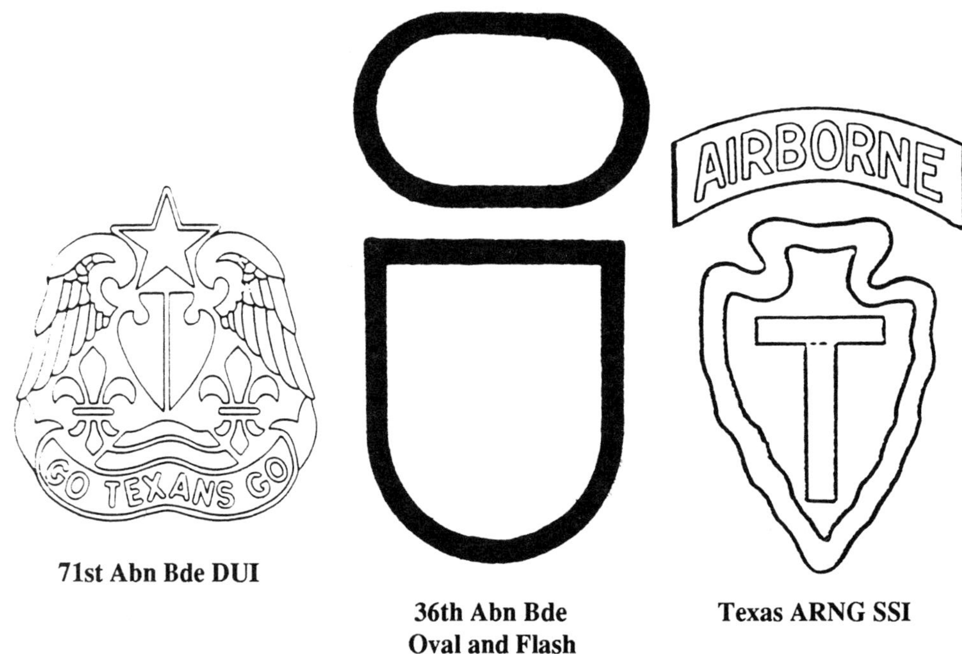

71st Abn Bde DUI

**36th Abn Bde
Oval and Flash**

Texas ARNG SSI

1968	**HHC, 1st Battalion, 36th Infantry Brigade** (TXARNG) consolidated with **HHC** and **Company B, 7th Battalion, 112th Armor Regiment** (TXARNG). The consolidated unit designated as **HQ Company, 71st Airborne Brigade (Separate)**. Assigned to the Texas ARNG. Activated at Houston, Texas.
1971	Reorganized and redesignated as the **71st Airborne Brigade**.
1973	Redesignated as the **36th Airborne Brigade**.
1978	Inactivated at Houston, Texas.
1980	Converted and redesignated as **HHC, 386th Engineer Battalion**.

HHC, 173d Airborne Brigade

173d Abn Bde Oval

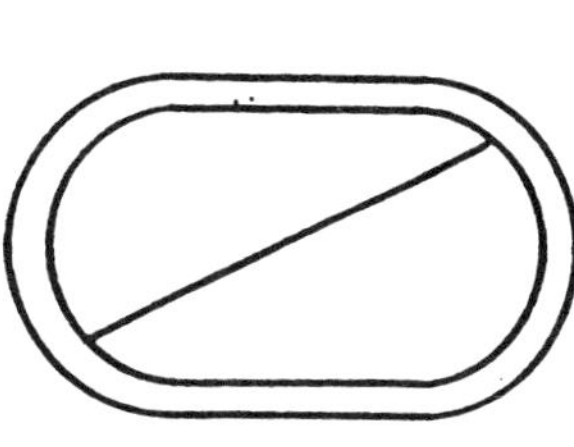

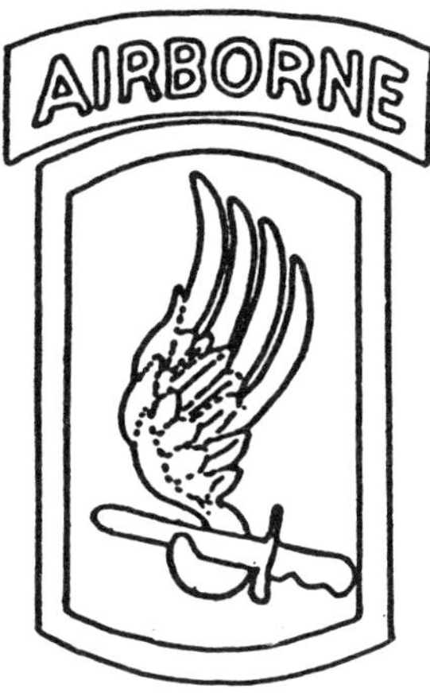

173d Abn Bde DUI

173d Abn Bde Oval
Unauth RVN variation

173d Abn Bde SSI

1917	Constituted in the National Army as **HQ, 173d Infantry Brigade.** Assigned to the **87th Division.** Organized at Camp Pike, Arkansas. World War I Campaign Participation provided a Streamer without inscription.
1919	Demobilized at Camp Dix, New Jersey.
1921	Reconstituted in the Organized Reserves as **HHC, 173d Infantry Brigade.** Assigned to the **87th Division.** Organized at Mobile, Alabama.
1925	Redesignated as **HHC, 173d Brigade.**
1936	Redesignated as **HHC, 173d Infantry Brigade.**
1942	Converted and redesignated as the **87th Reconnaissance Troop** (less 3d Platoon), Assigned to the **87th Division.** (**HHC, 174th Infantry Brigade** concurrently converted and redesignated as the **3d Platoon, 87th Reconnaissance Troop**). Ordered into Active Military Service. Reorganized at Camp McCain, Mississippi. Redesignated as the **87th Cavalry Reconnaissance Troop.** Assigned to the **87th Infantry Division.**
1943	Reorganized and redesignated as the **87th Reconnaissance Troop, Mechanized.** World War II Campaign Participation included the **Rhineland, Ardennes-Alsace** and **Central Europe.**
1945	Inactivated at Fort Benning, Georgia.

1947	Redesignated as the **87th Mechanized Cavalry Reconnaissance Troop.** Activated at Birmingham, Alabama.

1947   Redesignated as the **87th Mechanized Cavalry Reconnaissance Troop.**
Activated at Birmingham, Alabama.

1949   Reorganized and redesignated as the **87th Reconnaissance Company.**

1951   Inactivated at Birmingham, Alabama.

1963   Converted and redesignated (less the 3d Platoon), as **HHC, 173d Airborne Brigade**

The **3d Platoon, 87th Reconaissance Company** hereafter follows a separate lineage).
Relieved from assignment to the **87th Infantry Division.**
Concurrently withdrawn from the Army Reserve and allotted to the Regular Army.
Activated at Okinawa.

1965   Deployed to the Republic of Vietnam.

Vietnam Campaign Participation included the **Defense; Counteroffensive; Counteroffensive Phases II, III, IV, V, VI and VII; Tet Counteroffensive; Tet/69 Counteroffensive; Summer-Fall 1969; Winter-Spring 1970;** the **Sactuary Counteroffensive;** and **Consolidation I.**

1968   **Meritorious Unit Commendation (Army)**, with Streamer embroidered **VIETNAM 1965-1969**, awarded to **HHC, 173d Airborne Brigade.**

1971   Republic of Vietnam **Cross of Gallantry with Palm**, with Streamer embroidered **VIETNAM 1965-1970**, awarded to **HHC, 173d Airborne Brigade.**

1972   Redeployed and inactivated at Fort Campbell, Kentucky.
Personnel absorbed within the **101st Airborne Division (Airmobile).**

1973   Republic of Vietnam **Civic Action Honor Medal, First Class**, with Streamer embroidered **VIETNAM 1969-1971**, awarded to **HHC, 173d Airborne Brigade.**

1979   **Presidential Unit Citation (Army)**, with Streamer embroidered **DAK TO**, awarded to **HHC, 173d Airborne Brigade.**

HHC, 525th Military Intelligence Brigade (CEWI) (Airborne)

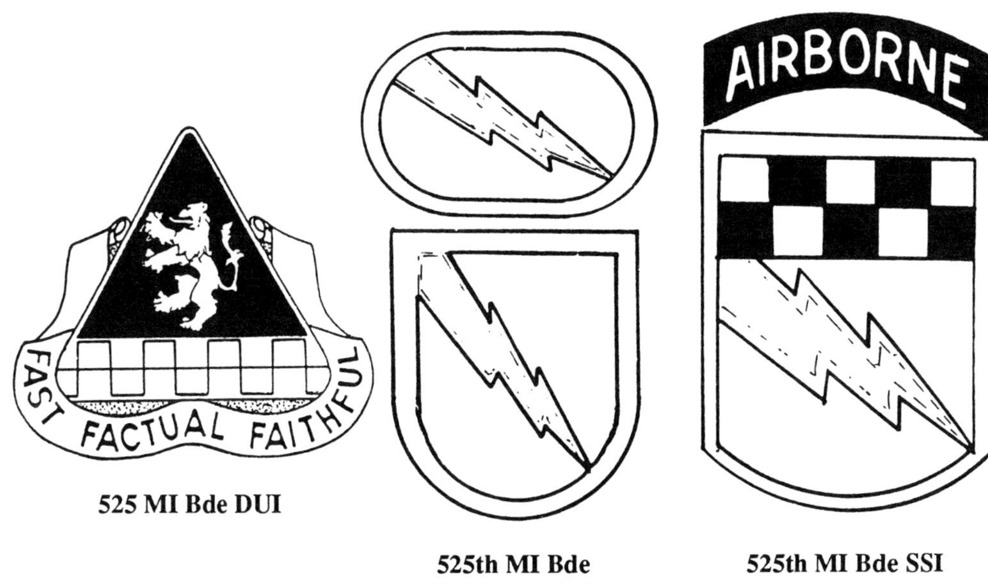

525 MI Bde DUI

**525th MI Bde
Oval and Flash**

525th MI Bde SSI

1946	Constituted in the AUS as the **525th Military Intelligence Group.** Organized at Heidelberg, Germany. Assigned to US Forces, European Theater.
1957	Relocated to Fort Meade, Maryland.
1964	Relocated to Fort Bragg, North Carolina.
1965	Deployed to the Republic of Vietnam. Vietnam Campaign Participation included **Defensive; Counteroffensive; Counteroffensive Phases II, III, IV, V, VI** and **VII; Tet 69/Counteroffensive; Summer-Fall 1969; Winter-Spring 1970; Sanc tuary Counteroffensive** and **Consolidations I** and **II.**
1973	Redeployed, and inactivated at Oakland, California.
1979	(**Forces Command Intelligence Group** reorganized and redesignated as the **18th Combat Intelligence Group (Provisional)** in 1971, then reorganized and redesignated as the **525th Military Intelligence Group (Corps) (Airborne)** in 1979. Relocated to Fort Bragg, North Carolina. Assigned to XVIII Airborne Corps.
1982	Reorganized and redesignated as the **525th Military Intel Gp (CEWI).**
1983	Deployed with elements of **XVIII Airborne Corps** to Grenada. Redeployed to Fort Bragg, North Carolina.
1985	Reorganized and redesignated as the **525th Military Intelligence Brigade (CEWI) (Abn).**

HHC, Aviation Bde, 82d Abn Division

82d Avn Bde DUI

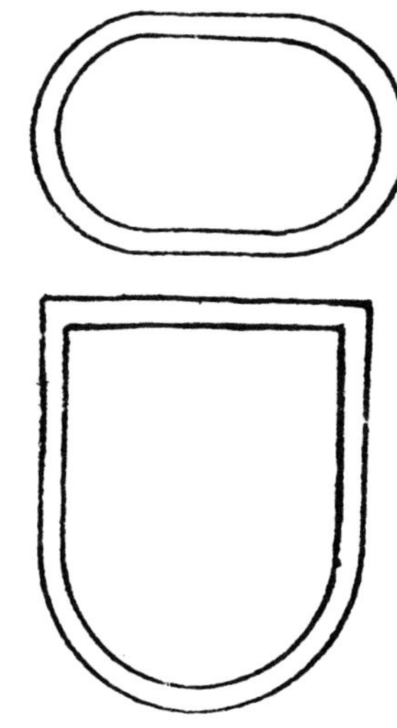

HHC, 82d Avn Bde
Oval and Flash
1988

82d Abn Div SSI

1986	Constituted as **HHC, Aviation Brigade**
	Allotted to the Regular Army.
	Assigned to the **82d Airborne Division.**
1987	Activated at Fort Bragg, North Carolina.

HHC, Avn Bde, 101st Abn Div (Air Asslt)

101st Avn Bde DUI

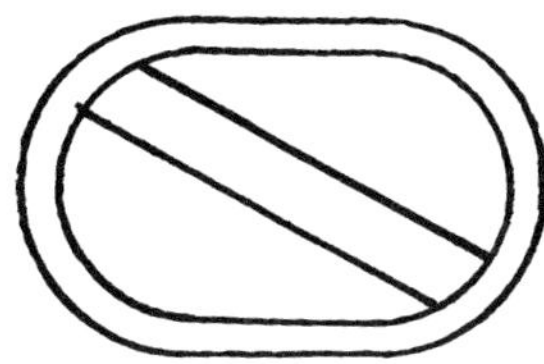

101st Avn Bde Oval
1988

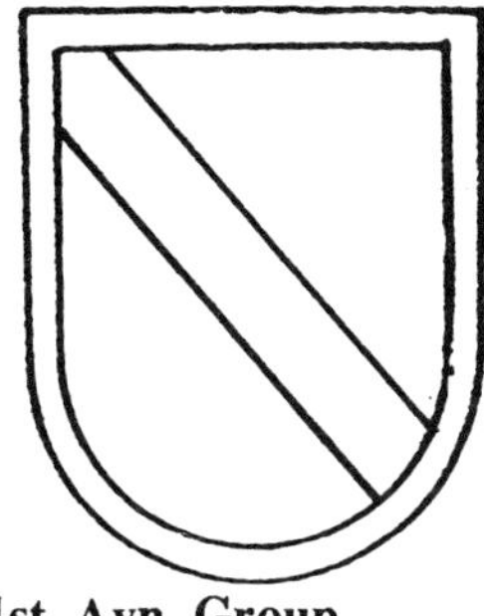

101st Avn Group
(Air Assault) Flash

101st Abn Div (AA) SSI

1968	Constituted as **HHC, 160th Aviation Group.** Allotted to the Regular Army. Assigned to the **101st Airborne Division.** Activated in the Republic of Vietnam. Vietnam Campaign Participation included **Counteroffensive Phases V, VI and VII; Tet 69/ Counteroffensive; Summer-Fall 1969; Winter-Spring 1970; Sanctuary Counteroffensive;** and **Consolidations I and II.**
1969	Redesignated as **HHC, 101st Aviation Group.**
1970	Republic of Vietnam **Cross of Gallantry with Palm,** with Streamer embroidered **VIETNAM 1968-1969,** awarded to **HHC, 101st Aviation Group.**
1971	**Valorous Unit Award,** with Streamer embroidered **THUA THIEN PROVINCE,** awarded to **HHC, 101st Aviation Group.** Republic of Vietnam **Civic Action Honor Medal First Class,** with Streamer embroidered **VIETNAM 1968-1970,** awarded to **HHC, 101st Aviation Group.**
1986	Reorganized and redesignated as **HHC, Aviation Brigade.** Assigned to the **101st Airborne Division (Air Assault).**

ABBREVIATIONS

A

Abn	Airborne
AIR	Airborne Infantry Regt
ARCOM	Army Reserve Command
ARNG	Army National Guard
Assoc	Association
AUS	Army of the United States
Auth	Authorized
Avn	Aviation

B

Bde	Brigade
BG	Brigadier General
Bn	Battalion

C

Cav	Cavalry
CEWI	Communications and Electronic Warfare Intelligence
Cmd	Command
Co	Company
CONUS	Continental United States
CONUSA	Continental United States Army
COSCOM	Corps Support Command
CPL	Corporal
CPT	Captain

D

DCSOPS	Deputy Chief of Staff for Operations
Div	Division
DUI	Distinctive Unit Insignia

E

Eng(r)	Engineer
ETO	European Theater of Opns

F

FA	Field Artillery

G

GIR	Glider Infantry Regt
Gl	Glider
Gp	Group

H

HHB	HQ and HQ Battery
HHC	HQ and HQ Company
HHD	HQ and HQ Detachment
HHSC	HQ, HQ and Service Company
HHT	HQ and HQ Troop
HQ	Headquarters
HSC	HQ and Service Company

I

In	Infantry
Inf	Infantry

L

Lt	Lieutenant
LTC	Lieutenant Colonel
LTG	Lieutenant General

M

Maint	Maintenance
MG	Major General
MI	Military Intelligence
MP	Military Police
MUSARC	Major US Army Reserve Command

N

NCBU	Non Color Bearing Units

O

OCONUS	Outside of the Continental United States
OD	Ordnance

P

Para	Parachute/Parachutist
PFC	Private First Class
PIR	Parachute Infantry Regt
PVT	Private

Q

QM	Quartermaster

R

RC	Reserve Componets (includes both ARNG and USAR)
RDJTF	Rapid Deployment Joint Task Force
Regt	Regiment
RVN	Republic of (South) Vietnam

S

SC	Signal Corps
SF	Special Forces
SGM	Sergeant Major
SOF	Special Operations Forces
SSI	Shoulder Sleeve Insignia
SUPCOM	Support Command

T

TDA	Tables of Distribution and Allowances.
Tng	Training
TOE	Tables of Organization and Equipment

U

Unauth	Unauthorized
USAR	United States Army Reserve

W

WWI	World War I
WW II	World War II

1SG	First Sergeant

LINEAGE TERMINOLOGY

ACTIVATE   To activate, following constitution, through assignment of personnel.

ALLOT   Assigning an organization to the active or reserve component of the US Army.

ARMY COMPONENTS
     The active army, Army National Guard and the US Army Reserve.

ARMY NATIONAL GUARD
     Army elements of the various states. Identified as the National Guard prior to 1954, with the word 'Army' added with the advent of the Air National Guard. Army National Guard in the service of the United Staes (ARNGUS), are thoseARNG units in active Federal status.

ARMY OF THE UNITED STATES
     Until 1920, applied solely to the Regular (active) Army, then expanded to include the National Guard whilst mobilized in the service of the United States (NGUS), and the Organized Reserves. In 1941, units activated without mobilization missions, were assigned to the AUS. In 1950, under the Army Re organization Act, the AUS became synonymous with the word 'Army', (as during 1920 through 1941).

ARMY RESERVE   The reserve forces of the US Army have followed the following progression:
- 1916   Designated as the Organized Reserves
- 1948   Redesignated as the Army Reserve Corps
- 1952   Redesignated as the (US) Army Reserve

ASSIGN   To become integrated into a larger organizational element.

CONSOLIDATE   To combine two or more units, retaining the lineage and heritage of each unit.

CONSTITUTE   By direction of the Secretary of the Army, the placement of designated units on the official Army rolls.

CONVERT   Rebranching and redesignating a unit. (ie; an Armor units is changed to Infantry).

DEMOBILIZE   The inactivating and removal from the official Army rolls prior to WW I.

DESIGNATE   The official title, (or numerical designation and name) of a unit.

DISBAND   The inactivation and removal from the official Army rolls after WW I.

INACTIVATE   To change from active to inactive status, remaining on the official Army rolls.

NATIONAL ARMY   Assigned elements of the military force as authorized on 18 May 1917.

NATIONAL GUARD   Changed to Army National Guard in 1954 when the Air National Guard was formed.

ORGANIZE   The assignment of personnel and equipment to a unit.

RECONSTITUTE   Restore to the official rolls of the Army, retaining former lineage, history and honors.

REDESIGNATE   Change the numerical designation or title of a unit, retaining lineage and honors.

REORGANIZE   Change the structure or type of unit. (ie from Infantry to Airborne Infantry)

INDEX

17th Airborne Division | (See Airborne Divisions)

18th Airborne Division | (See Airborne Divisions)
18th Aviation Brigade | (See Aviation Brigades)
18th Field Artillery Brigade | (See Artillery Brigades)

21st Airborne Division | (See Airborne Divisions)
22d Field Army Spt Cmd | (See Support Command)
24th Infantry Division | (See Infantry Divisions)
29th Infantry Regiment | (See Infantry Regiments)

35th Signal Brigade | (See Signal Corps Brigades)
35th Signal Group | (See Signal Corps Groups)

36th Airborne Brigade | (See Airborne Brigades)
37th Air Transport Battalion | (See Air Transport Battalions)
44th Air Transport Battalion | (See Air Transport Battalions)

48th Engineer Combat Regiment | (See Engineer Regiments)
48th Engineer Regiment | (See Engineer Regiments)

71st Airborne Brigade | (See Airborne Brigades)
71st Infantry Brigade | (See Infantry Brigades)

72d Air Transport Company | (See Air Transport Companies)

78th Cavalry Reconnaissance Troop | (See Cavalry and Reconnaissance Units)
78th Division | (See Divisions)
78th Division (Training) | (See Training Divisions)
78th Mechanized Cavalry Troop | (See Reconnaissance Units)

78th Reconnaissance Company | (See Reconnaissance Units)
78th Reconnaissance Troop | (See Reconnaissance Units)
78th Reconnaissance Troop Mechanized | (See Reconnaissance Units)

80th Airborne Division | (See Airborne Divisions)
80th Airborne Reconnaissance Company | (See Reconnaissance Units)
80th Airborne Reconnaissance Platoon | (See Reconnaissance Units)
80th Cavalry Reconnaissance Troop | (See Cavalry and Reconnaissance Units)

80th Division | (See Divisions)
80th Division Quartermaster Train | (See Divisions)
80th Division Train | (See Divisions)
80th Division (Training) | (See Training Divisions)

80th Infantry Division | (See Infantry Divisions)
80th Reconnaissance Company | (See Reconnaissance Units)
80th Reconnaissance Troop | (See Reconnaissance Units)
80th Reconnaissance Troop, Mechanized | (See Reconnaissance Units)

82d Airborne Division | (See Airborne Divisions)
82d Division | (See Divisions)
82d Infantry Division | (See Infantry Divisions)

84th Airborne Division | (See Airborne Divisions)
84th Division | (See Divisions)
84th Division (Training) | (See Training Divisions)
84th Infantry Division | (See Infantry Divisions)

86th Division | (See Divisions)
86th US Army Reserve Command | (See US Army Reserve)

88th Glider Infantry Battalion | (See Infantry Battalions)

97th Division | (See Divisions)
97th US Army Reserve Command | (See US Army Reserve)

100th Airborne Division | (See Airborne Divisions)
100th Division | (See Divisions)
100th Infantry Division | (See Infantry Divisions)

101st Airborne Division | (See Airborne Divisions)
101st Division | (See Divisions)

108th Airborne Division | (See Airborne Divisions)
108th Division (Training) | (See Training Divisions)
108th Infantry Division | (See Infantry Divisions)

112th Armor Regiment | (See Armor Regiments)
120th US Army Reserve Command | (See US Army Reserve)
135th Airborne Division | (See Airborne Divisions)

155th Anti-Aircraft Artillery Battalion | (See Artillery Battalions)
155th Brigade | (See Brigades)
155th Infantry Brigade | (See Infantry Brigades)

156th Brigade | (See Brigades)
156th Infantry Brigade | (See Infantry Brigades)

159th Brigade | (See Brigades)
159th Infantry Brigade | (See Infantry Brigades)

160th Infantry Brigade | (See Infantry Brigades)
173d Airborne Brigade | (See Airborne Brigades)

235th Engineer Battalion | (See Engineer Battalions)
235th Engineer Combat Battalion | (See Engineer Regiments)
235th Engineer Combat Regiment | (See Engineer Regiments)

269th Aviation Battalion | (See Aviation Battalions)

305th Ammunition Train | (See Ammunition Trains)
305th Engineers | (See Engineer Regiments)
305th Supply Train | (See Supply Trains)

309th Airborne Engineer Battalion   (See Engineer Battalions)
309th Ammunition Train   (See Ammunition Trains)
309th Engineer Battalion   (See Engineer Battalions)
309th Engineer Combat Battalion   (See Engineer Battalions)
309th Engineer Regiment   (See Engineer Regiments)
309th Supply Train   (See Supply Trains)

317th Troop Carrier Group   (See Troop Carrier)

325th Ammunition Train   (See Ammunition Trains)
325th Airborne Engineer Battalion   (See Engineer Battalions)
325th Engineer Battalion   (See Engineer Battalions)
325th Engineer Combat Battalion   (See Engineer Battalions)

351st Civil Affairs Command   (See Special Operations Forces)
386th Engineer Battalion   (See Engineer Battalions)

405th Quartermaster Battalion   (See Quartermaster Battalions)
405th Quartermaster Regiment   (See Quartermaster Regiments)

409th Quartermaster Battalion   (See Quartermaster Battalions)
409th Quartermaster Regiment   (See Quartermaster Regiments)

425th Quartermaster Battalions   (See Quartermaster Battalions)
425th Quartermaster Regiment   (See Quartermaster Regiments)

440th Troop Carrier Groop   (See Troop Carrier)
445th Chemical Det (NBC Recon)(SF)   82
460th Parachute Field Artillery Battalion   (See Artillery Battalions)
463d Parachute Field Artillery Battalion   (See Artillery Battalions)

501st Parachute Battalion   (See Parachute Battalions)
501st Parachute Infantry Regiment   (See Infantry Regiments)

502d Parachute Infantry Battalion   (See Infantry Battalions)
502d Parachute Infantry Regiment   (See Infantry Regiments)

503d Parachute Infantry Battalion   (See Infantry Battalions)
503d Parachute Infantry Regiment   (See Infantry Regiments)

504th Parachute Infantry Battalion   (See Infantry Battalions)
504th Parachute Infantry Regiment   (See Infantry Regiments)

506th Airborne Field Artillery Battalion   (See Field Artillery Battalions)
506th Parachute Field Artillery Battalion   (See Field Artillery Battalions)
506th Field Artillery Battalion   (See Field Artillery Battalions)

509th Combat Team   (See Combat Teams)
509th Parachute Infantry Battalion   (See Infantry Battalions)

516th Air Transport Company   (See Air Transport)

517th Combat Team	(See Combat Teams)
517th Parachute Infantry Regiment	(See Infantry Regiments)
522d Military Intelligence Brigade	(See Military Intelligence Brigades)
522d Military Intelligence Group	(See Military Intelligence Groups)
550th Glider Infantry Battalion	(See Infantry Battalions)
551st Parachute Infantry Regiment	(See Infantry Regiments)
596th Airborne Engineer Company	(See Engineer Companies)
780th Airborne Ordnance Maint Company	(See Ordnance Companies)
780th Ordnance Battalion	(See Ordnance Battalions)
780th Ordnance Light Maint Company	(See Ordnance Companies)
780th Ordnance Maintenance Company	(See Ordnance Companies)
784th Airborne Ordnance Maint Company	(See Ordnance Companies)
784th Ordnance Battalion	(See Ordnance Battalions)
784th Ordnance Light Maint Company	(See Ordnance Companies)
784th Ordnance Maint Company	(See Ordnance Companies)
800th Airborne Ordnance Maint Company	(See Ordnance Companies)
800th Ordnance Battalion	(See Ordnance Battalions)
800th Ordnance Light Mainte Company	(See Ordnance Companies)
800th Ordnance Maintenance Company	(See Ordnance Companies)
808th Airborne Ordnance Main Company	(See Ordnance Companies)
808th Ordnance Battalion	(See Ordnance Battalions)
808th Ordnance Maintenance Company	(See Ordnance Companies)
876th Aviation Engineer Bn	(See Engineer Battalions)
877th Aviation Engineer Bn	(See Engineer Battalions)
878th Aviation Engineer Bn	(See Engineer Battalions)
905th Field Artillery Battalion	(See Field Artillery Battalions)
905th Glider Field Artillery Battalion	(See Field Artillery Battalions)
909th Airborne Field Artillery Battalion	(See Field Artillery Battalions)
909th Field Artillery Battalion	(See Field Artillery Battalions)
909th Parachute Field Artillery Battalion	(See Field Artillery Battalions)
925th Airborne Field Artillery Battalion	(See Field Artillery Battalions)
925th Field Artillery Battalion	(See Field Artillery Battalions)
925th Glider Field Artillery Battalion	(See Field Artillery Battalions)
931st Signal Corps Battalion	(See Signal Battalions)
1128th Engineer Combat Group	(See Engineer Groups)
1277th Engineer Combat Battalion	(See Engineer Battalions)
1278th Engineer Combat Battalion	(See Engineer Battalion)

A

ARNG	(see US Army National Guard)
Adams, Paul D	8

AIR ASSAULT
> **DIVISIONS**

11th Air Assault Division	5, 8, 15, 18-20, 73, 74
1st Brigade	19
2d Brigade	20
3d Brigade	20
101st Airborne Div (Air Assault)	6, 20, 73-82, 90

AIR FORCE

9th Air Force	5
Air Force Bases	
McCook Field, Ohio	1
Stout Field, Indiana	4
Air Infantry	1

AIR TRANSPORT
> **COMMAND**

Air Transport Command	4

> **BRIGADE**

10th Air Transport Brigade	5, 6

> **BATTALIONS**

37th Air Transport Battalion	5
44th Air Transport Battalion	5

> **COMPANIES**

72d Air Transport Company	5
516th Air Transport Company	5
Airborne Center	6, 10, 18, 21

AIRBORNE
> **ARMIES**

First Airborne Army	7, **(65)**
First Allied Airborne Army	7, 8, 21, 22, **(65)**

> **COMMAND**

Airborne Command	2, 4, 7, 9, 21, 22, 73, 75, **(65, 70)**

> **CORPS**

1st Airborne Corps (UK)	7
XVIII Airborne Corps	(iii), 5, 6, 8, 11-12, 14, 16, 73, 75, 67, 81, 84 85, 89, **(66, 68, 71)**
XVIII Corps (Airborne)	5, 7, 8, 11-12, **(66)**

> **DIVISIONS**

6th Airborne Division (UK)	11,
6th Airborne Division	4, 63, **(66)**
9th Airborne Division	4, 63, **(66)**
11th Airborne Division	4, 5, 15, 18-20, 73, **(66, 71)**
Cmd and Control Bn	18, 19, **(665**
HQ and HHC	
1st Brigade	19
2d Brigade	20
3d Brigade	20

13th Airborne Division	4, 5, 15, 21, **(67)**
15th Airborne Division	4, 15
17th Airborne Division	4, 5, 9, 11, 15-16, 21, **(67)**
18th Airborne Division	4, 63, **(67)**
21st Airborne Division	4, 63, **(67)**
80th Airborne Division	5, 8, 17, 23-29, 55, 57, **(67)**
HQ, 80th Abn Division	23
HQ Co, 80th Abn Div	24
Recon Platoon	55
Recon Troop	55
82d Airborne Division	(iii), 4, 5, 6, 8, 12, 15-16, 17, 30-38, 73, 74, 76, 90, **(67, 68, 70)**
HHC, 82d Airborne Div	30-31
HQ, 82d Airborne Div	30-38
HQ Troop, 82d Abn Div	32
Cmd and Control Bn	33
1st Brigade	32-33
HHC, 1st Brigade	32-33, **(70)**
2d Brigade	8, 34-35
HHC, 2d Brigade	34-35, **(70)**
3d Brigade	8, 16, 36-37
HHC, 3d Brigade	36-37, **(70)**
4th Brigade	16, 38
HHC, 4th Brigade	38, **(70)**
84th Airborne Division	5, 17, 39-44, **(67)**
HQ, 84th Airborne Div	39
100th Airborne Division	4, 5, 17, 45-49, **(67)**
HQ, 100th Airborne Div	45
HQ Co, 100th Abn Div	46
101st Airborne Division	1, 4, 5, 6, 9, 15, 16, 17, 50-57, 73, 74, 76, **(67-68)**
HHC, 101st Abn Div	51-57, **(70)**
HQ, 101st Abn Div	50-57
1st Brigade	6, 16, 52-53, 73
HHC, 1st Brigade	52-53, **(70)**
2d Brigade	8, 54-55
HHC, 2d Brigade	54-55, **(70)**
3d Brigade	8, 56-57
HHC, 3d Brigade	56-57
108th Airborne Division	4, 5, 17, 58-62, **(67)**
HQ, 108th Airborne Div	58-62
135th Airborne Division	4, 5, 63, **(67)**

<u>**BRIGADES**</u>
      1st Airborne Infantry Brigade   15, 73
      1st Brigade (Abn), 1st Cav Div   73, 77-78, **(68, 70, 72)**
      1st Brigade (Abn), 8th Inf Div   73, 79, **(71, 72)**

      2d Airborne Infantry Brigade   73, 76, **(72)**
      2d Independent Para Bde (UK)   7

      36th Airborne Brigade   73, 86, **(71, 72)**
      71st Airborne Brigade   73, 86, **(69)**
      173d Airborne Brigade   6, 73, 81, 87-88, **(68, 70, 72)**

<u>**REGIMENTS**</u>
      <u>**Airborne Infantry**</u>
      187th Airborne Infantry Regt   5, 73
      188th Airborne Infantry Regt   5
      503d Airborne Infantry Regt   5

      504th Airbortne Infantry Regt   5, 73
      505th Airborne Infantry Regt   5, 73
      509th Airborne Infantry Regt   73
      511th Airborne Infantry Regt   5
      <u>**Glider Infantry**</u>
      194th Glider Infantry Regiment   16
      <u>**Parachute Infantry**</u>
      501st Parachute Infantry Regt   2, 73, 76
          1st Bn, 501st Para Inf Regt   2
      502d Parachute Infantry Regt   2
          1st Bn, 502d Para Inf Regt   2

      503d Parachute Infantry Regt   2
          1st Bn, 503d Para Inf Regt   2
          2d Bn, 503d Para Inf Regt   2

      504th Parachute Infantry Regt   3
      505th Parachute Infantry Regt   16
      507th Parachute Infantry Regt   16
      508th Parachute Infantry Regt   73, 76

      509th Parachute Infantry Regt   16, 73
          1st Bn, 509th Para Inf Regt   16, 73
          2d Bn, 509th Para Inf Regt   5
          3d Bn, 509th Para Inf Regt   5

      511th Parachute Infantry Regt   15
      517th Parachute Infantry Regt   7, 15
      551st Parachute Infantry Regt   7
          1st Bn, 551st Para Inf Regt   7
<u>**BATTALIONS**</u>
      <u>**Airborne Infantry**</u>
      550th Airborne Infantry Bn   7
      <u>**Glider Infantry**</u>
      88th Glider Infantry Battalion   2
      550th Glider Infantry Battalion   2

        <u>Parachute</u>

1st Parachute Battalion	1, 4
501st Parachute Battalion	1, 2, 15

        <u>Parachute Infantry</u>

501st Parachute Infantry Battalion	2, 3, 4
502d Parachute Infantry Battalion	2, 3, 4
503d Parachute Infantry Battalion	2, 3, 4
504th Parachute Infantry Battalion	2, 3, 4

<u>AIRBORNE TASK FORCE</u>

1st Airborne Task Force	7, **(66)**

Airborne Center	6, 10, 18, 21
Airborne School	10
Airborne Troop Carrier Command	(see Troop Carrier Command)

AIRMOBILE

    <u>DIVISIONS</u>

1st Cavalry Division (Airmobile)	5, 6, 77, 89
1st Brigade	6, 77
101st Airborne Div (Airmobile)	6, 53, 55
1st Brigade	53
2d Brigade	55
3d Brigade	57

America's Guard of Honor	16

AMMUNITION TRAINS

305th Ammunition Train	25
309th Ammunition Train	41
325th Ammunition Train	47

ARMIES

    <u>AIRBORNE</u>

First Airborne Army	7, **(65)**
First Allied Airborne Army	7, 8, 21, 22, **(65)**

    <u>BRITISH</u>

Second Army	11

    <u>UNITED STATES</u>

First US Army	8, 14, 23, 45, 58, **(65)**
Second US Army	8, 23, 45, 58, **(65)**
Third US Army	12, 13, 58, **(65)**
Fourth US Army	8, 13, 39, **(65)**
Fifth US Army	8, 39, 45, **(65)**
Sixth US Army	8
Seventh US Army	58
US Army Pacific	13

ARMOR

    <u>CORPS</u>

II Armored Corps	8, 11

    <u>DIVISIONS</u>

4th Armored Division	17

C

8th Infantry Division	5, 9, 11, 12, 73, 79, **(68)**
1st Brigade, 8th Inf Div	5, 73, 79, **(71, 72)**
24th Infantry Division	5, 73, **(68, 71, 72)**
2d Brigade, 24th Inf Div	5, 73
36th Infantry Division	73
71st Infantry Division	73
78th Infantry Division	11, 34-35, 36, **(67)**
80th Infantry Division	5, 17, 23-29, 57
HQ Company, 80th Inf Div	24
82d Infantry Division	16, 17, 30-38
84th Infantry Division	5, 17, 39-44
85th Infantry Division	80
86th Infantry Division	11
87th Infantry Division	16, 88
97th Infantry Division	11
100th Infantry Division	5, 17, 45-49
HQ Company, 100th Inf Div	45
101st Infantry Division	15, 17, 50-57
108th Infantry Division	4, 5, 17, 58-62, 63
HQ Company, 108th Inf Div	58, 59

<u>REGIMENTS</u>

29th Infantry Regiment	1

<u>BRIGADES</u>

1st Infantry Brigade	75
2d Infantry Brigade	76
36th Infantry Brigade	86
71st Infantry Brigade	86
155th Infantry Brigade	34-35, 36
156th Infantry Brigade	34, 36-37
159th Infantry Brigade	55, 56
160th Infantry Brigade	54, 56-57
169th Infantry Brigade	80
173d Infantry Brigade	87, **(68, 70, 72)**
174th Infantry Brigade	87

Infantry School	2
Iron Duke	6
Irvin Parachute Company	1
IX Engineer Command	(see Engineers)

J

Johnson, James H. Jr	19
Joint Special Operations Command	19

K

L

M

S

U

W

X

Y

"UTRINQUE PARATUS"

About the Author

Geoffrey T. Barker, a native born Englishman, served as a British paratrooper in Europe and the Middle East. After moving to the United States, he enlisted as a paratrooper in the U S Army, spending most of his career with US Army Special Forces. Between Special Forces assignments he served with the 82d and 101st Airborne Divisions; XVIII Airborne Corps; 8th Infantry Division; 1st Corps Support Command; and HQ RCPAC. He was assigned to the 82d Airborne Division during the Dominican Republic crisis. His first assignment to Southeast Asia was with the 1st Brigade, 101st Airborne Division, later serving two tours as a military assignee to the Central Intelligence Agency. During his first assignment with the CIA, he was commissioned as a First Lieutenant of Infantry . He retired as a Lieutenant Colonel, Special Forces. His last four year assignment was as a Division Chief with the ACofS G-3/DCSOPS, 1st Special Operations Command, Fort Bragg NC. During his military career, in addition to his forty-two awards and decorations, he was the recipient of the US Army Combat Infantryman Badge, the Special Forces Tab and the Master Parachutist Badge. His foreign awards include the German Army Expert Infantryman Badge and Shooting Ropes, the Republic of Vietnam Army Ranger Badge, the Royal Thai Army Special Forces Aguillette; and eight foreign parachute qualification badges. Since retirement from the US Army, he accepted an appointment to Colonel, as Chief of Staff of the North Carolina State Defense Militia, vacating this position to move to Florida, where he is a senior research staff member, under a Department of Defense contract to the US Special Operations Command, MacDill Air Force Base. He and his wife Judy live in Hillsborough County, Florida. They are both avid campers.

AIRBORNE ASSOCIATIONS

Many airborne associations change addresses annually as their presidents are elected annually for the following year. A comprehensive, and current list of airborne associations and chapters may be found in the monthly publication - **Static Line,** Box 87518, College Park, Georgia 30337.

The following permanent Airborne Association National Headquarters will advise of Association Chapters covering your area of residence:

82d Airborne Division Association	**101st Airborne Division Association**
PO Box 1442	PO Box 345
Bloomington, IN 47402	Sweetwater, TN 37874

Volume 1   A Concise History of US Army Special Operations
                  Forces.   ISBN 0-922004-00-5

Volume 2   A Concise History of the US Airborne Army, Corps,
                  Divisions and Brigades.   ISBN 0-922004-01-3

Future editions in progress:

Volume 3   A Concise History of US Army Airborne Infantry
                                             ISBN 0-922004-02-1

Volume 4   A Concise History of US Army Airborne Long Range
                  Patrol and Long Range Survellance Units.
                                             ISBN 0-922004-03-X

Volume 5   A Concise History of US Army Airborne Artillery
                                             ISBN 0-922004-04-8

Volume 6   A Concise History of US Army Airborne Armor,
                  Aviation and Cavalry.   ISBN 0-922004-05-6

Volume 7   A Concise History of US Army Airborne Combat
                  Support.   ISBN 0-922004-06-4

Volume 8   A Concise History of US Army Airborne Combat
                  Service Support.   ISBN 0-922004-07-2

A Concise History of US Army Special Operations Forces

by Geoffrey T. Barker (LTC SF Ret)

With an Introduction by **Lieutenant General (USA Ret) William P. Yarborough**

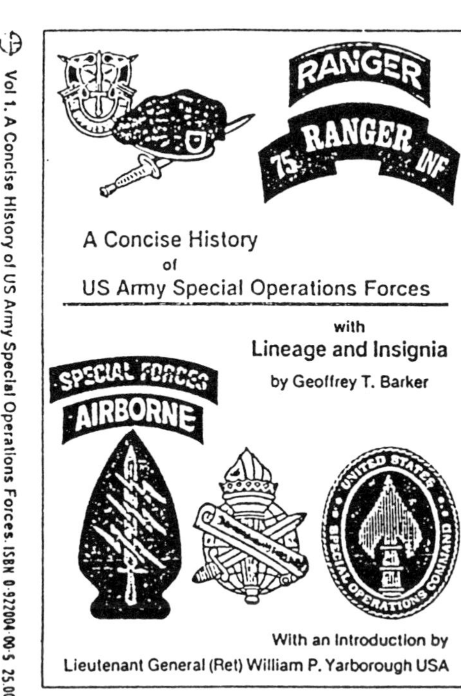

INCLUDES

Discussion of **OSS** units.

Data of **Military Government** units and early **Special Forces Detachments.**

HISTORY, LINEAGE and INSIGNIA of:

SPECIAL OPERATIONS COMMANDS
(1st SSF, USSOCOM, 1st SOCOM, JFKSWCS, 1st SFOD-Delta, SOCEUR, SOCCENT, SOC-K, SOCLANT, SOCPAC & SOCSOUTH).

US ARMY CIVIL AFFAIRS
(3 CA Cmds; 10 CA Bdes; 21 CA Groups; 2 CA Bns & 37 CA Cos)

SPECIAL OPERATIONS AVIATION, ASA/MI, MEDICAL, CHEMICAL, SIGNAL and SUPPORT

US ARMY RANGERS
(6 Ranger Bns - WW II; 75th Ranger Regt; 35 Ranger Companies)

US ARMY PSYCHOLOGICAL OPERATIONS
(4 PSYOP Groups; 13 PSYOP Battalions; 26 PSYOP Companies)

US ARMY SPECIAL FORCES
(1st Special Forces; 18 Activated SF Groups; 2 Separate SF Companies (Alaska & Thailand); MACV-SOG; CCN, CCC, CCS; FANK/UITG)

> "An outstanding reference for US Army SOF...truly outstanding:
> GEN James J. Lindsey, CINC USSOCOM
>
> "Superb, the Army has needed this"
> LTG Carl W. Stiner, CG XVIII Abn Corps

Volume 1 of the <u>Concise History Series</u> with 218 pages; **400 color and 1,000 black and white illustrations.**

$25.00 plus $1.50 postage/handling
DEALER RATES AVAILABLE
UPON REQUEST

NAME ____

ADDRESS____

_______________________________ ZIP __________

Anglo-American Publishing Company
Suite 196, 813 East Bloomingdale Avenue, Brandon, FL 33511